CW00394506

Counselling and the Holy Spirit

Counselling and the Holy Spirit

Peter Ledger

Marshall Pickering

Marshall Morgan and Scott
Marshall Pickering
34-42 Cleveland Street, London W1P 5FB

Copyright © 1989 Peter Ledger.
First published in 1989 by Marshall Morgan and Scott
Publications Ltd
Part of the Marshall Pickering Holdings Group

ISBN: 0 551 01790 2

Text Set in Baskerville by Input Typesetting Ltd, London
Printed in Great Britain by Camelot Press, Southampton

Contents

To Pauline with love.

All Scripture references are taken from the New International Version of the Bible unless otherwise stated.

Foreword by Douglas McBain

I am very glad to introduce readers of this excellent book of counselling to the author, Peter Ledger. He is a good friend with whom I have shared many times in ministry both in England and overseas in India. Erudite though he is with an impressive academic background, Peter is essentially a pastor teacher in God's family. He is a man of the Spirit who is not afraid to enjoy life in the world. He has a reflective nature and an engaging turn of mind. Above all he is observant, quickly picking up not only the heart of an argument, but also its tones, its tensions and the significance of its silences too. Having seen him on the job, I could not think of another who could write more helpfully, yet without jargon, on the complexities of counselling today.

A first requirement of those who write about church ministries is adequate first-hand experience of life and growth at the level of local congregations. Lacking this, all books on theology or spirituality are as detached from reality as castles in the sky. If they emerge out of living experience the teaching takes wings, and its applications are immediately relevant for many other situations than the ones which gave it birth.

The first sign of genuine renewal in any church is always the warmth of its fellowship. Where once there was coolness and aloofness, now it is family life for the people of God. This is one reason why good renewal churches grow, and it also explains their magnetic quality to those who lives are disturbed by real personal stress. The sick, the needy, the depressed and the lonely will travel many a mile to find a place of warmth, light, affection and acceptance. Not that Brickhill Baptist Church is only composed of hundreds of the damaged. It is a lively, caring and a faithful church. They are always building there, planning for further growth. They are well led by an excellent team of full-timers in Brian Tibbert and Peter Ledger, and other brothers and sisters gifted and mature in counselling and cramming quarts of activity into pint pots of time available. Yet within this exciting situation there is such care for the needs of individuals. If ever I wanted to get a church to give long-term help to someone whose situation would not yield to straightforward and immediate solutions, I would think first of Brickhill.

You will be greatly blessed by Peter Ledger's book. It is a mine of wise counsel, a sure guide where there is darkness, confusion, fear or ignorance. He has drawn help from the best of the secular writers. He has also weighed up the contributions of those with spiritual insight. Having then worked it through with many down-to-earth situations among those with whom he regularly shares God's word, he knows the difference between theory and practice. So too will you with the help of this book, and the aid of the Holy Spirit. There is no situation too deep for the Spirit to reach. Every time He speaks to us our lives are made more whole and our hopes for the future rekindled. As we have received good counsel, we too will be equipped to counsel others. Happy indeed the church which has such a team of counsellors as the church from which this book emerges.

Acknowledgements

I am grateful to the many friends who have made the writing of this book possible:

to Douglas McBain, my editor, who persuaded me to try to write it and who has guided my way;

to the people of my first pastorate, Victoria Park Baptist Church in Bristol, upon whom I cut my pastoral teeth;

to the people of Brickhill Baptist Church in Bedford whose pastor I have been for twenty years now and amongst whom are so many hearts that care;

to all those who have trusted me enough to open their inner selves to me and to give me the privilege of counselling them;

to fellow pastors who have been so open and honest about the realities of counselling-care ministry in local churches today;

to Anne Todd who has so willingly typed the manuscript, and to her husband Dave who made the word-processor correct it;

to Pauline, my beloved wife and partner, who, as I sought to write, deflected so much that would have made the task impossible.

Finally, in the words of Psalm 16, I praise the Lord Who counsels me.

Explanations

They say that I am a preacher and I should preach more often; that as presiding elder I should lead more decisively; that I should create more teaching courses for the lambs and the sheep; that I should present more of the Lord's overall vision for the church. They are doubtless right. But then I see the prisoners: even when they are pretending to be free, I 'read' the hurt, the anxiety, the despair, the anger, the guilt, the aloneness which binds them, and my heart goes out to them. They need help commensurate with their need. They need informed Christian counselling. Many will receive it, if at all, in and through the local fellowship of Christians. If they are to receive it, we in the churches have some tough issues to address.

There is the issue of CONTEXT. For us church leaders or carers, the context for our people-helping ministry is that of the local fellowship: however, we have a range of involvements and commitments within the life of that fellowship as well as our being called to be witnesses beyond it. The vast majority of us are not and are not going to be full-time counsellors. Yet so few of the counselling books seem to recognize that: so few seem to be written by those who, as they write, are actually in local church leadership and dealing with the multi-faceted demands of such ministry in these days. Indeed, to pursue their commitment to counselling, some have had to move *out of* local church ministry – which only serves to underscore my point. Counselling is not the be-all and end-all of church life, as calls to prayer or evangelism or social protest constantly remind us. What we who are grass-roots leaders and carers need is help which understands how we are placed: help which enables us to perceive the rightful place of counselling in the overall mission–ministry of the Body of Christ; which understands our parameters of commitment, which recognizes the special overtones counselling has when both counsellor and counselee are part of the same worshipping community and its life.

There is the issue of STANCE. When you turn to the body of counselling literature, it is not so much the plethora of books that is the problem as the bewildering *variety* of counselling presuppositions, theories and methodologies advocated in those tomes. When, in his *Roots and Shoots*, Roger Hurding set out to trace the family-tree of counselling and psychotherapy, it took him over 400 pages to do so! We are all very much in his debt, but we are not thereby excused from taking up our own position. What *are* our Christian convictions concerning the ministry of counselling-care? How do we determine our attitude towards secular psychotherapy and its findings? By what principles shall we accept or reject counselling techniques or research or goals? Is counselling skill given or learned?

There is the issue of COMPASSION. 'His compassions, they fail not' – but what about ours? As the Spirit of Christ moves us outwards into a spiritually bankrupt society, we are going to gather its victims: the deserted, the despised, the rootless, the misfits – human beings deeply damaged and hungry for love. But there are so many. The demands upon our reservoir of compassion are already running at a high level. We need guidance: to help us release more of the counselling-care potential still locked away in the church; to tread the path between, on the one hand, being over-sympathetic and thus being strung along by those who crave attention but do not have any intention of being healed, and, on the other hand, being too quickly confrontational and, if the person does not respond, leaving him, hoping that he might go away – which he will; to sustain our own spirituality; and to care as Christ cared.

I hope that this book addresses such issues. I have sought to gather in a manageable format what needs to be tackled in the local fellowship – questions to be answered, resources to be exploited, practicalities to be considered. I aim to have produced a guide-book which any team of church leaders and any team of church carers-cum-counsellors might usefully work their way through. It is so often *through* those that care that the Lord heals the wounded.

Peter Ledger
1988

Section A

KEY QUESTIONS

1

How much of a local church priority is counselling care?

Although as she advanced towards me her eyes were flooding with tears, the radiance on her face indicated that she was crying for joy; when she reached me, she, a pensioner, embarrassed me, a fledgling minister, with her profusive thanks. All I had done was preach a sermon which insisted that the terrible evils of life are to be interpreted as consequences of the Fall, and not as 'acts of God' as our insurance policies call them. It transpired that more than 20 years previously, the only baby she had ever been able to carry in her womb was stillborn. She was a faithful Christian, and as her fellow believers had sought to minister to her, what she had heard amounted to this: 'we don't understand why God does these things, but He is sovereign, so we must bow our heads in submission to His will'. That 'message' she accepted with the surface of her mind – after all, she was a Christian, and the message was in terms of God – but rejected with her inner being where a deep hatred of the God who had killed her baby flared up out of the darkness of her despair. However, the whole weight of her upbringing had been such as to instil into her that any expression of anger, let alone hatred, was unthinkable, with the result that she suppressed her real feelings and carried on trying to be a conscientious servant of the Lord – which she had been doing joylessly, for over 20 years prior to that sermon. That Sunday morning, I saw a captive set free by the Lord Who is full of Grace and Truth, and I was called to be a counsellor. In addition to the

Ministry of the Word and Sacraments, I was to move along-side imprisoned people as the servant of the Counsellor Who opens prison doors. More than 25 years later, I continue to promote His counselling care in the local church context. This book is but part and parcel of that promotion – and to the same end, that He might set the captives free.

I had better define my terms: what is counselling care? As will become clear, I would not wish to separate counselling either from effective overall pastoral care organized by the leadership in the local church, or from that caring for and ministering to one another which is part and parcel of normal Christian living for those who are members one of another in the Body of Christ. However, this book is particularly to do with how the local church is to respond to people who are experiencing intense difficulties in some aspects of their emotions, thoughts and/or behaviour. I understand coun-selling care to mean a serious offer of appropriate help to such persons through a genuinely caring Christian relation-ship with them. In many instances, admittedly, all that the person may be seeking and will accept is 'first aid', a way of dealing with the current external problem; clearly that deci-sion must be respected, and such help can be quickly given. In other instances, however, the presented external difficulty is clearly symptomatic of an unexcavated underlying problem, the healing of which will require a more on-going and struc-tured counselling relationship. Nowadays, increasing numbers of people who are experiencing and presenting such problems find their way to our churches. However, the avail-able pastoral resources of a local church are usually limited, and the church leaders and nucleus members have many other Christian responsibilities demanding of their time, energy and commitment. It is that reality of stretched resources which raises the urgent question of priorities: how high on the Christian agenda should counselling be? It may be enormously difficult for us Christians to conceive of not responding readily to human need when it forces its attention upon us, yet there are too many Christian ministers who, already over-taxed with responsibilities, then themselves come apart at the seams because of the additional weight of others' personal problems being heaped upon them. What that says is that we need to view counselling care in a definitely Christian perspective. The revitalization of truly Christian perspectives by the Holy Spirit actually delivers to us what we need, for one of the major fruits of charismatic renewal thus far has been freshly to convince the People of God that their real considerations are not to be so much *church* as *Kingdom* oriented.

The People of God are rediscovering the Kingdom of God, are beginning to come to terms again with the core truth that the Kingdom of God is central for Jesus. For Him, all else is referred to the Kingdom just because it is *the* point of reference; all else finds its definition only by reference to the Kingdom. Whereas, for example, some Christians develop an unhealthy interest in tracking down and rooting out demons to the point that 'deliverance ministry' becomes an end in itself and gets out of all proportion, Jesus's perspective prevents such distortion: for Him, the expulsion of demons can be accomplished and interpreted only by reference to God and His Rule:

'if I drive out demons by the Spirit of God, then the Kingdom of God has come upon you' (Matthew 12.28).

The essential thing is not demons or their expulsion: the essential thing is the Kingdom of God.

The centrality of the Kingdom of God in the praying, thinking, teaching and doing of Jesus has, of course, been long recognized by theologians – for example, by Professor C. H. Dodd in his 'Parables of the Kingdom' first published as long ago as 1935. However, what had tended to be the possession of theologians is now becoming the passion of the People of God. That disturbing, fermenting breaking-in of the actual Ruling of God right into people's own lives through the ministry of Jesus, that same ruling of God can break through into *our* time and space, through Jesus Christ and by the Holy Spirit. God's sovereignty of Grace and Righteousness can penetrate our natural earthy sin-soaked humanity, washing, redeeming, changing it, can refashion a person's values and valuations and reform sinful human structures. God's Rule is a powerfully penetrative reality – like yeast tackling a batch of dough – hence the ferment in so many of our local churches or fellowships! The Spirit of Christ is once again weaning the

Christians off their obsession with *their* church – *its* ways, *its* tradition, *its* membership numbers, *its* buildings, *its* reputation – and onto the primary reality: *His Kingdom*, the arriving of the Ruling of God. Our Lord, by the moving of His Spirit, is making a play to repossess His own Church! By His grace and initiative, many congregations are redis-covering the very raison d'être of the local church, namely, to be an instrument of the Kingdom's arriving; to be, in the hand of God, an instrument with which He can penetrate man's here and now in order to redeem it. All of this says that the Church's priorities are to be the priorities of the Kingdom. The Kingdom priorities are modelled by the Person and the Ministry of Jesus. In order to view local church counselling care in true Christian perspective, we have first to set it firmly in the context of those Kingdom priorities which the life of Jesus embodied. The desire of the Church must surely be that her priorities are those of her Lord. So what are the priorities of Jesus? And where does counselling care stand in relation to them?

The kingdom priorities of Jesus

It is of cardinal importance that the local church seeks to live by her Lord's priorities, to identify which entails serious study of the Gospels, Acts and the Epistles. In the fellowship I lead, as we sought to discern the threads which go into the weaving of the whole mission-ministry of Jesus, we arrived at a list of 4 double-coloured ones thus: Prayer and Worship, Evan-gelism and Community Involvement, Teaching and Disci-pling, Healing and Pastoral Care. What we have been endeav-ouring to do in recent years, and are endeavouring to do still, is to work right into our church consciousness, life and planning the imperative that these are *always* to be our priorities just because they are the priorities of Jesus and of the New Testament Church, according to the Scriptures. Our first task therefore, is to attend to those Scriptures.

i) *Prayer and worship*
The Gospels afford us only relatively few glances through the window they open upon the devotional life of Jesus, but, even so, there is plenty of evidence that the lifting of His soul

and spirit in prayer and worship towards His Father was a cornerstone of His whole ministry. Luke, for example, portrays for us a Jesus Who is to be found seeking the Father's way and will in prayerful devotion prior to the major developments in His ministry: prior to the Spirit coming upon Him following His baptism (3.21), prior to His choosing of the Twelve (6.12), prior to the questions which brought Peter's confession (9.18), prior to His transfiguration (9.28), in Gethsemane, and on the Cross nearing death (22.44; 23.34 and 46). From the start, as His ministry grew in popularity causing Him to be constantly in demand, Luke reports:

'But Jesus often withdrew to lonely places and prayed' (5.16).

The Lucan record also portrays a Jesus Who teaches prayer to His disciples – for example, in the parables of 'The Persistent Friend' (11.5–10), 'The Importunate Widow' (18.1–8), and 'The Pharisee and the Tax Collector at Prayer' (18.10–14). The tantalizing sentence 'on the Sabbath day, He went into the synagogue as was His custom' (4.16) suggests that, as far as possible, public worship was an integral part of Jesus's life, as do His attendances at Jerusalem Festivals according to John, and His celebration of the Passover with His disciples. John's distillation of what is timeless Truth in and from Jesus includes major teaching on true worship as He encounters the Samaritan woman at Jacob's well (chapter 4), and His high priestly prayer (chapter 17).

Confirmation of the importance of prayer and worship to Jesus is that Luke (in Acts) portrays His Church as being a praying and worshipping Church from the beginning. There is the cameo of Acts 2.42 which tells us that the new Christians

'devoted themselves to the apostles' teaching and to the fellowship, to the breaking of bread and to prayer'.

From that base, according to Acts, there is ample evidence of prayer and worship woven into the very fabric of the early church's understanding and practice. There are momentous prayer meetings in the context of opposition (4.23–31), and momentous times of worship such as that in which Barnabas and Paul are discerned to be God's men for pioneer mission work (13.1–3). Deacons are commissioned by prayer (6.6), converts are prayed with that they might be filled with the Holy Spirit (8.14–17), Dorcas is raised from death by prayer (9.40), Gentiles are converted and baptized into the Church – a crucial step forward – just because both Cornelius and Peter were praying and hearing the Lord (10.9 and 30), elders are set apart by prayer to lead the infant churches (14.23), prison doors open following prayer and worship (16.25–26), and moving farewells are sealed by prayer (20.36–37 and 21.5–6). Paul's letters confirm the high profile of prayer and worship in the early church: there are his own marvellous prayers for the churches (Ephesians 1.15–19 and 3.14–21, for example), and in his first letter to the Christians in Corinth, as he attempts to correct imbalances and excesses, he gives us a splendid glimpse of the charismatic worship of the churches the Spirit brought to birth through his ministry. Paul's writings are also rich in exhortations to pray and to worship, witness these moving verses from Colossians chapter 3:

'Let the word of Christ dwell in you richly as you teach and admonish one another with all wisdom, and as you sing psalms, hymns and spiritual songs with gratitude in your hearts to God. And whatever you do, whether in word or deed, do it all in the name of the Lord Jesus, giving thanks to God the Father through him' (3.16–17).

All of this is eloquent testimony to the importance Jesus gave to prayer and worship in His own practice and in the teaching He gave to His disciples. Indeed, it is John's reading of Jesus that the Son says only what the Father tells Him to say (12.49–50) and does only what the Father shows Him to do (5.19–20). There is essential and continuing communion between the Son and His Father. We can only wonder at the wealth of meaning the single word 'Abba' ('Father') has upon the lips of Jesus. The weight of the Biblical evidence is decisive: movement towards God in prayer and worship was fundamental to Jesus, and at its heart, for all of His own

ministry and for all of theirs, stands the prayer He taught
His disciples:

'Abba, Father . . . Your Kingdom come'.

In terms of the Kingdom of God, prayer and worship are a
top priority.

ii) Evangelism and community involvement
Jesus is manifestly a man on an urgent mission. The essence
of His cry is:

'The time has come. The Kingdom of God is near. Repent
and believe the Good News!' (Mark 1.15).

When Jesus sends out the Twelve on mission, the central
instruction is:

'Go . . . to the lost sheep of Israel. As you go, preach this
message: "The Kingdom of heaven is near" ' (Matthew
10.6–7).

When Jesus sends out *seventy-two* other followers of His, the
same commission is given to them:

'Tell them: "the Kingdom of God is near you" ' (Luke
10.9).

As the good news is proclaimed in words, Jesus is confident
that God will reinforce it with mighty acts which demonstrate
to all present that the Kingdom of God is indeed near.
Accordingly, as He sends out the Twelve, to the injunction
to preach the good news of the Kingdom, He adds matter-
of-factly:

'Heal the sick, raise the dead, cleanse those who have
leprosy, drive out demons' (Matthew 10.8)!

Jesus preaches for decision. He declares that the God of all
grace and righteousness is penetrating the here and now of
human experience, attacking the powers of evil and man's

thraldom to sin, to offer a whole new way of being and living to those who will repent and believe and enter in under the loving sovereignty of Father God. To decide for this Kingdom message is the most important decision a person can ever make: it is worth anything he has – which is the thrust of the twin parables of the Hidden Treasure and the Precious Pearl (Matthew 13.44–46). It is a matter of life or death, heaven or hell, such that Jesus feels obliged to declare that it is better to enter the Kingdom maimed than it is to be whole but not to enter, for the latter condition leads only to hell (Mark 9.43–47). It is therefore imperative that the People of God get to hear the marvellous news of the Kingdom *now*. Individuals must hear and see and respond whoever they are, whether respectable Nicodemus or despised Zacchaeus. Communities must hear, too, and have opportunity to respond: Jesus clearly hoped that whole towns would embrace the good news, but, respond or not, they were to have their chance; so to the seventy-two, Jesus says:

> 'When you enter a town and are welcomed, eat what is set before you. Heal the sick who are there and tell them, "The Kingdom of God is near you". But when you enter a town and are not welcomed, go into its streets and say, "Even the dust of your town that sticks to our feet we wipe off against you. Yet be sure of this: The Kingdom of God is near" ' (Luke 10.8–11).

The cries of Jesus, 'Woe to you Korazin ... Bethsaida ... Capernaum' (Luke 10.13–15) show His disappointment that whole communities failed to respond to the good news. All of this demonstrates that evangelism is a top priority for Jesus. It is entirely characteristic of Him to say:

> ' "Let us go to the nearby villages so I can preach there also. That is why I have come". So He travelled throughout Galilee ...' (Mark 1.38–39).

It has to be said that evangelism and community involvement have often been held over against each other by different groups of Christians, although markedly less so in recent years. It has also to be said that they are inseparable in the ministry of Jesus in this sense, that calling individuals and their community to repentance and faith on the one hand, and seeking to meet their needs on the other, is all part and parcel of the same kingdom reality to Jesus. What Jesus preaches, embodies and demonstrates has radical implications for the community of Israel, and it is in that sense that we can speak of Jesus's involvement in the community. He is not a political activist, though some have wanted to make Him so: for example, He neither condemns nor resists the Roman occupation of Israel. However, He does progressively aggravate and then alienate the leaders of His own Jewish community, which only goes to show how deeply involved in and with that community He is. What He does in effect is to challenge the very values and presuppositions by which the community lived and organized itself.. It was axiomatic to the Jewish community as Jesus found it that God was on the side of privilege, respectability, wealth, authority and status. Conversely, to be materially, physically or socially disadvantaged was to be religiously disadvantaged: God was clearly not impressed by you. People were thus extremely unequal before God. Not to put too fine a point on it, this was a position which Jesus dynamited. He maintained that *all* were equally loved by Father God and that *anyone* who repented and believed could enter the Kingdom of God. Furthermore, the very things that were taken to betoken advantage in God's eyes, privilege, wealth and the like, were declared by Jesus to be more than likely to prove disadvantageous! So, for example, Jesus's experience in ministry leads Him to this conclusion,

'It is easier for a camel to go through the eye of a needle than for a rich man to enter the Kingdom of God' (Mark 10.25),

and to this one, put to chief priests and elders:

'I tell you the truth, the tax collectors and the prostitutes are entering the Kingdom ahead of you' (Matthew 21.31),

both facts of ministry which the parable of The Great Banquet underlines (Luke 14.15–24). Jesus went to considerable lengths to demonstrate to those who were deemed to be or deemed themselves to be disadvantaged or even disqualified before God (these often being collectively referred to in Scripture as 'the poor') that God's grace was as fully present and available to them as to anyone. He gives His special attention and acceptance to those considered beyond the pale: He seeks out and sits at table with tax collector Zacchaeus, He ministers understandingly to the woman taken in adultery, He defends and applauds the 'bad' woman who anoints Him with expensive perfume. He is good news for the poor:

'Blessed are you poor, for yours is the Kingdom of God' (Luke 6.20),

and bad news for the rich:

'But woe to you rich, for you have already received your comfort' (Luke 6.24).

To reach 'the poor', to release them from the supposed stigma of their poverty, to encourage them to see themselves as sons and daughters of God is a Kingdom imperative which Jesus enjoys. At some point along the way, such involvement on His part in the community was given a label; although intended to be a contemptuous slur upon His character, it may well have delighted Him as it now does us: they dubbed Him 'friend of tax collectors and sinners'. Jesus tried to meet people at their point of need, but He always saw God and His Kingdom as the answer to their needs. His community involvement and His evangelism were one.

The New Testament church, in reflecting these evangelism and community involvement priorities of Jesus, also holds them together. One cannot justifiably extract from the Acts or the Epistles a programme for local church evangelism as distinct from a local church programme for community involvement. They belong together. The first Christians are natural witnesses and evangelists. They take it as read that they are to spread the good news as Jesus did, and they do it both enthusiastically and effectively. The authorities' worst move, from their own point of view, was to execute Stephen and so scatter the Christians, for that had the effect of scattering natural witnesses: as Luke records it,

> 'Those who had been scattered preached the word wherever they went' (Acts 8.4).

Later on, the releasing of Barnabas and Paul into specific pioneer evangelism gave tremendous impetus to the spread of Christianity, and confirmed the priority of evangelism in the mind of the Church. In tandem with all of that, however, is the understanding that what the Spirit of Christ brings into being out of evangelism is *new community:* Christ-community within the larger community. From the beginning, the Christians desired and endeavoured to be the society of Jesus, embodying the values of the love of Jesus. The cameos of Acts 2.44–47 and 4.32–35, plus Paul's collection for the Jerusalem church during famine there, show, for example, that there was a Spirit-inspired sharing of goods and resources over against the divisions and inequalities of the world. Just that, really, is the community involvement of the infant churches – to be *Christian* communities within but over against the wider community. It is noticeable that Paul does not exhort the churches to mount evangelistic or social programmes, but that he does consistently and emphatically call the Christians to *be* Christ-like one to another, to *be* the Body of Christ, to bring forth the fruit of the Spirit. *Then* the Lord Himself will continue *His* mission-ministry through the churches, and maintain *His* Kingdom priorities of evangelizing and meeting needs: it is then that His disciples are salt and light to the world, as He desires.

iii) Teaching and discipling
Teaching and discipling carry a high profile in the mission-ministry of Jesus. He was so aware of how the Word of the Kingdom needed to be deeply worked into the minds, hearts and lives of those who followed Him. The parable of the Sower yields us the evidence that, in His own experience, many who began to respond to the Word subsequently fell away or were seduced away. Thus, teaching the truths of the Kingdom was an essential part of everyday ministry. The Gospels' testimony is of a Jesus Who was constantly 'teaching

and preaching' in synagogues, on the hillsides, by the sea-shore, wherever. It is a part of that testimony that His teaching impacted:

> 'The people were *amazed* at His teaching because He taught them as one who had authority, not as the teachers of the law' (Mark 1.22).

Once people had been drawn by the proclamation of the Kingdom and the urgency of responding to it, it seems that Jesus invested much of His time and energy in teaching those who would listen. The sermon on the mount in Matthew chapters 5 to 7 is a classic example. Jesus presents the radical nature of Kingdom life which men and women can grow into as the sovereign power of God enters them. In the Beatitudes (5.3–12), He teaches the values of the Kingdom; in the 'you have heard that it was said – but I tell you' antitheses of 5.21–48, He teaches the revolution which the Kingdom is to effect in the inner life; and in the sections concerning prayer, for example (6.5–15 and 7.7–11), He teaches practical guidelines for day to day discipleship. Jesus makes it clear that it is essential that His followers build their lives upon what He says – the sermon concludes with the parable of the Wise and Foolish Builders, the wise builder being the person 'who hears these words of mine *and puts them into practice*' (7.24).

The intention of the teaching ministry is to make disciples: according to Matthew 28.19–20, that is precisely what the first believers understood the mind of the risen Christ to be – 'make disciples, baptizing them . . . and teaching them to obey everything I have commanded you'. There are many instances where Jesus overtly connects His teaching with discipleship commitment – indeed, He often does it in a way calculated to halt men and women in their tracks and 'count the cost': one heart-stopping example will suffice:

> 'Large crowds were travelling with Jesus, and turning to them, He said: "if anyone comes to me and does not hate his father and mother, his wife and his children, his brothers and sisters – yes, even his own life – he cannot be my disciple. And anyone who does not carry his cross and follow me cannot be my disciple" ' (Luke 14.25–27).

14

There is also plenty of evidence to show that Jesus gave priority to teaching and discipling the Twelve in particular (or, perhaps, a larger core-group of whom the Twelve are the up-front nucleus). That was true from the early Galilean ministry:

'When he was alone, the Twelve and the others around him asked him about the parables. He told them, "The secret of the Kingdom of God has been given to you . . ." ' (Mark 4:10–11),

right through to the journey to Jerusalem and death:

'They left that place and passed through Galilee. Jesus did not want anyone to know where they were, because He was teaching His disciples' (Mark 9.30–31).

That is also John's understanding of the pattern of the ministry, for he places the climax of the whole teaching and discipling ministry of Jesus in the Upper Room where Jesus is alone with the Twelve; there, He teaches them much, conveying the heart of discipleship to them, as, for example:

'A new command I give you: Love one another. As I have loved you, so you must love one another. By this all men will know that you are my disciples, if you love one another' (John 13.34–35),

and:

'This is to my Father's glory, that you bear much fruit, showing yourselves to be my disciples' (15.8).

It is clear that the first Christians discerned this teaching-discipling priority and carried it over into the life and practice of the New Testament church. From the beginning, new Christians 'devoted themselves to the apostles' teaching' (Acts 2.42) and what is often insufficiently recognized in relation to the mission-ministry of Paul is his emphatic commitment to teaching and discipling consequent upon pioneer evangelistic

15

work. He spends time nurturing infant Christian communities whenever he can. To the Ephesian elders he can say:

'You know that I have not hesitated to preach anything that would be helpful to you, but have taught you publicly and from house to house' (Acts 20.20) 'for three years' (20.31).

Acts 14.21–22 is typical:

'Then Paul and Barnabas returned to Lystra, Iconium and Antioch, *strengthening the disciples and encouraging them* to remain true to the faith'

– Lystra and Iconium being dangerous places for Paul to revisit! Paul's letters themselves, as he writes to the churches he established, are a living memorial to the priority he gave to working to root and ground young disciples in the things of Christ.

iv) Healing and pastoral care

Throughout His ministry, Jesus healed many people. What leaps to mind immediately are His healings of leprosy, paralysis, blindness and the like, but it is essential for us to recognize that the healing given by Jesus is multi-faceted, being by no means limited to *physical* healing. Frequently, Jesus detected other layers of need behind the physical symptoms presented to Him, or bondages of other kinds than physical. In the celebrated episode of Mark 2.1–12, the man lowered through the roof to Jesus is paralysed, yet Jesus says to him:

'Son, your sins are forgiven'.

Jesus perceives a *spiritual* bondage to break, which is the key to his healing. In Mark 9.14–29, Jesus is presented with a child who is deaf and dumb, and who suffers from epileptic fits, but Jesus discerns a *demonic* bondage, breaks its hold, and the child is physically restored. Similarly, the Gerasene demoniac (Mark 5.1–20) is healed mentally, emotionally and socially. So already we see the healing ministry of Jesus reaching beyond the physical and into the realms of emotional, mental, spiritual and behavioural healing, all of which are very much the province of counselling. Furthermore, in other instances, there are no physical symptoms being presented at all, yet the nature of Jesus's ministry is deeply healing. A classic is that of Zacchaeus (Luke 19.1–10). When this wealthy but ostracized chief tax collector declares:

> 'Look Lord! Here and now I give half of my possessions to the poor, and if I have cheated anybody out of anything, I will pay back four times the amount',

we are listening to a man who has been most deeply healed. Jesus responds:

> 'Today salvation has come to this house',

an apt moment for us to remind ourselves that healing and saving are closely related. We may choose to translate Luke 7.50 'your faith has *saved* you' and Luke 18.42 'your faith has *healed* you', but the Greek is exactly the same. Zacchaeus is saved and healed.

Closely associated with His healing activity, Jesus is the embodiment of pastoral care to those who are to a real extent open to Him. The synoptists can but record this movingly:

> 'When he saw the crowds, he had compassion on them because they were harassed and helpless, like sheep without a shepherd' (Matthew 9.36).

> 'A man with leprosy came to him and begged him on his knees: "if you are willing, you can make me clean". Filled with compassion, Jesus reached out his hand and touched the man. "I am willing. Be clean!" ' (Mark 1.40–41).

> 'When the Lord saw her' (the widow of Nain whose only son has died), 'his heart went out to her and he said: "Don't cry." '. He then raised her son back to life (Luke 7.13–15).

This is the caring Jesus Who gives bread to the hungry, Who comes to the aid of His Twelve when they are rowing against a contrary wind and getting nowhere, Who is concerned to

17

complete the inner healing of a woman who touched him clandestinely, Who defends the woman criticized for anointing Him lavishly with expensive perfume, Who gives dignity and hope back to a woman caught in adultery but being used as a pawn by His enemies, Who rescues His disciples from the embarrassment of failing to heal a child, Who calms them as they quarrel because James and John have an eye on the best seats in heaven, Who ministers assurance to doubting Thomas and forgiveness and restitution to Peter who had denied even knowing Him. Each of those Gospel encounters is a vintage vignette of pastoral counselling and care. They cannot be divorced from healing: for Jesus, healing and pastoral care are one, a Kingdom priority and an integral part of Kingdom being.

This healing and care ministry continues in and through the New Testament church. In the early formative days, Peter and John, by the Name of Jesus, heal the cripple at the gate called Beautiful (Acts 3.1–10), the infant church prays that the Lord will stretch out his hand to heal (Acts 4.30), people brought their sick out into the streets in the hope that Peter's shadow might fall on them (Acts 5.15), and it is reported of Philip's ministry in Samaria:

'With shrieks, evil spirits came out of many, and many paralytics and cripples were healed' (Acts 8.7).

'Signs and wonders' were an integral part of the pioneering ministry of Paul and Barnabas, and those included healings – witness the physical healing of the cripple at Lystra (Acts 14.8–10) and the spiritual healing of the slave girl at Philippi (Acts 16.16–18). In his letters, Paul makes it very clear that, by the power of the Spirit, such deeds accompanied his preaching and were vital in bringing new churches to birth: hence his reminder to the Christians in Corinth about his first visit there:

'My message and my preaching were not with wise and persuasive words, but with a demonstration of the Spirit's power, so that your faith might not rest on men's wisdom, but on God's power' (1 Corinthians 2.4–5).

Paul quite naturally lists 'gifts of healing by the Spirit' in the representative list of charismata he gives in 1 Corinthians 12.7–11. Healing quite clearly retained in the early church the high profile it had in the ministry of Jesus.

The same holds true of pastoral care. Some of the practical caring exhibited by the early church I have already described in the Community Involvement section, and we shall see in greater detail in Chapter 4 that the dominical commandment 'to love one another' is one which Paul, particularly, greatly expands upon and forcefully insists upon as he writes to the churches, so there is no need at this juncture to illustrate the undoubtedly caring nature of the early Christian community. It will suffice to quote what Tertullian knew to be a common saying among pagans: 'See how these Christians love one another'.

Which of the kingdom priorities takes priority?

I have sought to establish that prayer and worship, evangelism and community involvement, teaching and discipling, and healing and pastoral care are the major threads woven together to make up the mission-ministry of Jesus, but which of the threads dominates? Which Kingdom priority comes first? I have written "prayer and worship" first – does that indicate precedence? This was a question to which our Bedford fellowship addressed itself in concerted prayer, and what came through to establish itself as of first importance was one of those so simple pictures, by which the Spirit conveys the mind of Christ to the church. There were lots of pictures, scriptures and "words", but the one picture stood, stayed and grew while the rest faded. It was the picture of a factory floor arranged to a definite plan, the essential features being that firstly, it was composed of four workshops, each equal in area; and secondly, each workshop was open to the others at the centre, the plan being thus: (see page 20).

The message was and is that *none* takes priority over the others: rather, all take priority in the church together. This is particularly important because there is a tendency in the charismatic renewal scene (and, indeed, outside it) to follow a 'flavour of the month' pattern. Now the all-important word is 'prayer', but then it becomes 'evangelism'; now it is

Prayer and Worship	Evangelism and Community Involvement
Teaching and Discipling	Healing and Pastoral Care

'teaching', and then it becomes 'healing'. It may well be that we have to give particular attention to a particular Kingdom activity because we have neglected it, but they are all 'top priority' for the church, and are to remain so all the time. Confirmation of that for us came through a second picture which also grabbed our attention from amongst the many others. It was a picture of that kind of children's roundabout which is apparently known as a 'Witch's Hat'! It has seats which are suspended from the top of a central pole and which are joined together around the pole. In the picture, when too many children clambered onto one seat leaving the others vacant, the roundabout tilted out of balance and failed to operate effectively, but when the children dispersed themselves onto all the seats, the roundabout functioned beautifully. The meaning or Word, was crystal-clear: it is unhealthy to over-emphasize any one Kingdom priority at the expense of the others. Perhaps I should list them in a different order each time I mention them, in order to emphasize that they are all of equal priority. Ideally, I need to do the impossible, namely, to say or write them all at the same moment! The fact is that, although we can trace the coloured threads which go into the weaving of Christ's ministry, that ministry is actually a seamless robe. It is only as all the threads give themselves together to the overall design that the grace and truth and glory of the whole are revealed.

The place of counselling in the local church

As we have seen, counselling is altogether part and parcel of healing and pastoral care. It is, therefore, a true Kingdom priority, which means that, on the one hand, it may hold its head high, but, on the other hand, it may not hold its head higher than the other Kingdom priorities. Counselling care needs to have its own place by right on the agenda and in the life of the local church but it should not dominate. Church leaders need to ensure that the Kingdom priorities are being held in *balance* in the goals and activities of the fellowship, and that counselling care and inner healing do not fall victim to either under-emphasis or over-emphasis.

The danger of under-emphasis

Where too little or no real counselling care is being offered by the local church, many real needs are not met: inner emotional and mental anguishes stay buried in the depths, but they are buried *alive* and are liable to break out under pressure. Such difficulties, unresolved, militate against the person concerned being able to worship and/or to establish or sustain trusting relationships with brothers and sisters in Christ and/or to know the peace and the joy of salvation and/or to grow towards that wholeness which Christ is and gives. In too many Christian contexts, there is too little honesty in respect of doubts and difficulties. One major obstacle is the notion that it is somehow a shocking thing for a believer to have doubts, to feel depressed, to be in difficulty. This is nonsense. Scripture itself is well peopled with men of God who cry out to the Lord or to fellow-believers concerning the inner turmoil they are experiencing, plus the spiritual crisis it is engendering. Such a frankness is surely the lasting appeal of many a Psalm, a powerful example being Psalm 22 with its opening cry:

'My God, my God, why have you forsaken me?
Why are you so far from saving me,
so far from the words of my groaning?'

and with the way in which a man of faith feels himself to be being ripped to pieces by 'bulls', 'lions', 'dogs', 'wild oxen' and 'evil men'. In what are often referred to as his 'Confessions', the prophet Jeremiah models utter frankness before God and men – witness the day he cries out to his God:

'O Lord, you deceived me, and I was deceived!' (Jeremiah 20.7),

and to the world in general:

'Cursed be the day I was born!' (20.14).

The magnificent outpourings of Job yield a further telling example. Even more significantly, the same surely holds true for Jesus: His temptations are real temptations, the obduracy of Scribes and Pharisees and the dullness of disciples provoke cries of frustration from Him, the anguish of Gethsemane has depths we cannot plumb, and the dereliction of His being made sin for us upon the Cross forced from His lips the cry of Psalm 22. It is essential that Christians *own* rather than deny their emotions and thoughts when they are in turmoil. However, it is devastating for someone to own the feelings he has, having been encouraged to do so, only to discover that there is no-one who will really listen to and take seriously what he needs to share, and no-one who can show him what to do with the thoughts and emotions he is now owning. We shall explore this whole area when we consider a counsellor's 'toolkit' in chapter 5. Suffice it to say at this juncture that there are too many Christians who want to help the troubled, but who have not disciplined themselves to listen, who are not yet in real contact with even their own thoughts and emotions, and who thus are quite *unable* to help those who need help. A local community of Christians surely needs to include those who can offer competent counselling care in the Name of Jesus: where real needs are being really taken seriously, the Kingdom can advance.

The danger of over-emphasis
It is absolutely clear that it is not Jesus's intention that we should be predominantly pre-occupied with ourselves. All

four Gospels carry a version of His profound pronouncement that the person who is intent upon preserving his own life will lose it, whereas he who lets go of his pre-occupation with self and focuses upon Him will find his true identity and have more abundant life. We must beware, therefore, lest we produce Christians who concentrate mainly upon themselves, who are intent upon taking their own spiritual temperature day by day, and, if the reading is fractionally up or down, upon seeking the counsel of Christian allies almost as a reflex action. This essentially self-centred kind of discipleship (albeit with a spiritual gloss) can be unwittingly fostered if, for example, we permit 'fads' to direct church caring. If the 'healing of memories' is all the rage, then the danger is that our folk will focus upon their own history and try to come up with some memory which needs healing! Alternatively, if pastoral visiting of members is elevated above the call to prayer or to evangelism or to discipleship, then what comes into being is a church which members evaluate only in terms of how well or otherwise they themselves are being looked after. One of the essential challenges the Spirit has brought to the church today, be it old denominational or new restor-ationist, is the Word from the Lord (I first heard it through John Wimber): 'I want My Church back'. Many of us so badly needed to be delivered from the 'my' church syndrome to the 'His' church truth. When it is 'my church', then pastoral care and counselling relate to *me*; when it is 'His church', to *Him*. The Lord seeks to heal me not simply for my own sake, but that I may relate with Him, walk with Him, work for Him, and be an integral part of that Body through which He continues His Kingdom mission-ministry. So I feel the need urgently to tell myself and advise you to see counselling-care ministry always in the perspective of the Kingdom: it is then a ministry which keeps us fit for the other Kingdom ministries of prayer and worship, evangelism and community involvement, teaching and discipleship, all of which point us away from ourselves and to the intention of our Lord. 'Seek *first* the Kingdom of God'.

2

What is the theology underlying your counselling ministry?

Whilst it is gloriously true that charismatic renewal has galvanized us with the rediscovery of the marvellously imma-nent Father, Son and Spirit, it is also true that it can bring in its wake an impatience with all theology and all wrestling with the deep things of God. It is profoundly liberating to be worshipping and serving the Lord with so much more *heart*, for Christianity's expression in our land has for too long been too cerebral. However, Jesus Himself confirms that our privilege-cum-responsibility is to love the Lord our God with all of our heart *and* with all of our *mind*. Yes, we can most certainly do without the aridity and rationalistic liberalism of much academic theology and its pretensions, but no, we dare not capitulate to any pressure to reduce all Christian verities to naive and simplistic childishness: the Lord would have us be child*like*, not child*ish*. We must give our mind to a theology of counselling, 'theology' in its living sense of purposeful, empowering Word from God. We need a soundly theological basis for our counselling because our basis determines two issues of utmost importance in the counselling context, being those of *expectation* and *culpability*.

The matter of expectation

The whole matter of expectation is one which the Christian community and, probably, society at large should be taking far more seriously than is presently the case. In regard to

24

counselling care, a key factor is what expectations are actually in play: the counsellor has expectations, but then so has the counselee. So what are they? And, Christianly, what should they be?

Former ages, of course, recognized the power of expectation. In the 1720's, for example, Alexander Pope published what he termed the ninth Beatitude, being the cynical assertion:

'Blessed is he who expects nothing, for he shall never be disappointed',

matched in its disenchantment by Richard Whateley's maxim:

'It is folly to expect men to do all that they may reasonably be expected to do'.

William Shakespeare comes to our rescue, however, with a far more balanced perspective in *All's Well That Ends Well*:

'Oft expectation fails, and most oft there
Where most it promises; and oft it hits
Where hope is coldest and despair most fits'.

Failed expectations can propel us into darkness, yet, being brother to hope, expectation can also be a shaft of light into our private dungeons. It is one of the great God-created flavours of our humanity, but as such it needs true counsel and direction: false expectation is a curse, right expectation a blessing; too high an expectation is like a millstone around your neck, but then so is expectation which is too low; and any expectation outraged is trouble. A man returned to our local church after a lapse of some years during which, unbeknown to him, the church's worship had markedly changed through a new inflow of the Spirit: as I went to greet him, he flung at me in accusatory tones the question 'What have you done to my church?' That was not a great piece of theology, but it does speak volumes to the issue of expectation: he was *expecting* one thing, actually found a very different thing, was thrown by that, and became very angry. The way through was to explore his expectation. *Why* was he expecting what he was expecting? When looked at face on, was his expectation founded upon truth, reality, sound reason? Was it, as I much prefer to put it, *Christian*? That little episode initiated a pastoral counselling situation. However, what we need to see is that each counselling situation *of itself* raises its own 'expectations' issue in any case. As we embark upon a counselling relationship, what do *I* the counsellor *expect* of it? What set of expectations or level of expectation am *I* conveying to the counselee? With what expectations of counselling or of me does *he* begin? In the context of Christian counselling, the expectation level and content are determined by what the counsellor and counselee *believe*. Too many would-be counsellors do not realize that, and give it no particular thought. The question a Christian counsellor needs to address and, indeed, live with, is: are my counselling ministry expectations rooted and grounded in the Truth which Christ is? Are they *Christian*? At this point in our study, therefore, let us give our minds to the securing of a sound, theological, biblical stance towards the issue of counselling expectation.

In chapter one, focused upon the centrality to Jesus of the Kingdom of God, we set pastoral counselling very firmly in the perspective of the overall Kingdom priorities of Jesus Himself. What we must now do is to invite Jesus to give us *His* parameters for our expectations for ministry in His Name.

Parameter 1: Jesus teaches that there is a rich NOW for Kingdom disciples
The revolutionary Word which Jesus preaches, teaches and Himself embodies is:

'The time has come. The Kingdom of God is near. Repent and believe the good news' (Mark 1.15).

Rather than being preserved for the End Time beyond history, the Kingdom of God is near NOW – 'near' not in the sense that it has not quite arrived; rather, in the sense that it has arrived, it is here and now, right alongside, but what yet remains is for men and women to embrace it with repentance and faith. They will then know the reign of God in their lives, and will be a living part of His Kingdom People in the here and now. As seed in the earth, as yeast in the dough, as salt in the vegetables, so the Kingdom is penetrating and permeating the present, producing new life, finer texture, fuller flavour, NOW. The *verbs* of this NOW are clear and crisp:

towards God, to repent, to have faith, to pray (ask, seek, knock), to hear, to obey;

towards people, to love, to give, to be merciful, to forgive, to bless, to serve, to do good;

towards self, to deny and to humble.

These verbs delineate the Kingdom Way, commitment to which makes you 'blessed'. The word is *makarios*, used, for example, in the Beatitudes ('blessed are . . .'); it describes those who are in a 'happy' condition because God undertakes to meet their needs and to bestow upon them the benefits of His salvation. Says Jesus:

'He who comes to me will never go hungry, and he who believes in me will never be thirsty' (John 6.35)

and:

'I have come that they may have life, and have it to the full' (John 10.10).

In Him, in the Kingdom, there is life which satisfies man's deepest longings, which persuades him, which engages his potential, which gives him a real person to be – and, as Jesus indicates to Peter, which richly rewards him:

'I tell you the truth, no-one who has left home or wife or brothers or parents or children for the sake of the Kingdom of God will fail to receive many times as much in this age and, in the age to come, eternal life' (Luke 18.29–30).

Jesus offers a really rich NOW, a new NOW, strong in grace, righteousness and truth, and rich in satisfaction: a NOW so strong and satisfying that if a person chanced to stumble upon it, like treasure in a field, he would give his all to have it.

All of that said, we must also come to terms with this, that Jesus clearly seeks to alert His troops to recognize that the NOW He gives is subject to attack by the enemy, by flesh-world-devil opposition to God's reign and ways. Jesus warns against the fleshly pull towards hating, lusting and seeking revenge, and against the hypocrisy, pride, self-preoccupation and the love of money and reputation evident in Pharisees and Scribes. He implores His followers not to be sucked into the world's vortex of desiring the best position or being 'top-dog':

'Not so with you. Instead, whoever wants to become great among you must be your servant, and whoever wants to be first must be slave of all' (Mark 10.43–44).

He roundly declares

'You cannot serve God and Money' (Luke 16.13),

and just because the temptation to try is so strong, and many succumb to it, He returns to the money theme frequently. He bids those who go out in His Name to discern and to expel the demons and unclean spirits which are enslaving many people. As Peter seeks to dissuade Jesus from taking the Way of the Cross, He x-rays what is really happening, as He says: 'Get behind me *Satan*!' and later, following that most sombre of statements, 'Satan entered Judas', Jesus says:

'Simon, Simon, Satan has asked to sift you as wheat. But I have prayed for you, Simon, that your faith may not fail' (Luke 22.31–32).

So the tentacles of flesh, world and devil are always menacingly seeking to establish a spoiling hold upon that NOW which God gives to those who come in under His reign.

Parameter 2: Jesus teaches that there is also a richer NOT YET that awaits Kingdom disciples
When Jesus says to His disciples:

> 'I tell you the truth, some who are standing here will not taste death before they see the Kingdom of God come with power' (Mark 9.1),

and:

> 'I say to you that many will come from the east and the west, and will take their places at the feast with Abraham, Isaac and Jacob in the Kingdom of heaven' (Matthew 8.11),

and, at the Last Supper,

> 'I tell you the truth, I will not drink again of the fruit of the vine until that day when I drink it anew in the Kingdom of God' (Mark 14.25),

then it is clear that the Kingdom of God as seen by Jesus is *also* a decisive future event: there is marvellous consummation yet to be. Some of His parables confirm that in graphic ways: the parables of the Ten Virgins, the Talents, and the Sheep and Goats, which Matthew has gathered together (chapter 25), all look to a decisive future event; the Bridegroom will arrive, the Master will return, the Son of Man will come in all His glory. What we taste NOW is real Kingdom fare, yet it is but an hors d'oevre before the main meal, the messianic banquet in the Kingdom of heaven. The full unfolding of God's Kingship and its implications for humankind is yet to come. It is an integral part of the Kingdom teaching of Jesus to urge men and women not to miss that, not to exclude themselves from it, but rather to watch, pray and be ready.

The significance of the Cross

It is time for us to remind ourselves that the mission-ministry of Jesus is always, as it were, waiting for the Cross. Most truly, from the moment of His conception to the moment of

His ascension, the saving event of Jesus Christ is all one, but it is the cutting edge of His death and resurrection which breaks the stranglehold of sin, evil and death, and which enables the releasing of the power of the Holy Spirit upon and into whoever believes. By the will of God, the Spirit applies the work of Christ to the believer, giving the gift of the NOW *and* the guarantee of the NOT YET of the salvation He brings. Only post-Easter and post-Pentecost can the reality and the richness of both NOW and NOT YET dawn and be apprehended through faith. It therefore becomes the task of the other New Testament writers to find ways of expressing both, and of holding them together in terms of Christian understanding. The first Epistle of John does that in succinct summary form:

> 'How great is the love the Father has lavished on us, that we should be called children of God! And that is what we are! The reason the world does not know us is that it did not know him. Dear friends, now we are children of God, and what we will be has not yet been made known. But we know that when he appears, we shall be like him, for we shall see him as he is. Everyone who has this hope in him purifies himself, just as he is pure' (1 John 3.1–3).

NOW we are children of God: what we will be is NOT YET known, but we can be sure that it will be so tremendous as to beggar description and defy language!

Crucially for the ministry of counselling, the concrete implications of the NOW-and-NOT-YET nature of Christian discipleship are made plain in the Scriptures by the way of direct comment upon the situation New Testament Christians find themselves in. I illustrate from the Epistle to the Philippians.

Firstly, Paul makes it patently clear that Christ has made him a new person, given him a new person to be and more and more fully to become, here and now:

> 'For to me, to live is Christ. . . .' (1.21).

> 'But whatever was to my profit I now consider loss for the sake of Christ. What is more, I consider everything a loss

compared to the surpassing greatness of knowing Christ Jesus my Lord . . .' (3.7–8).

'I know what it is to be in need, and I know what it is to have plenty. I have learned the secret of being content in any and every situation, whether well fed or hungry, whether living in plenty or in want. I can do everything through him who gives me strength' (4.12–13).

'And my God will meet all your needs according to his glorious riches in Christ Jesus' (4.19).

There is a very substantial Christian NOW.

Secondly, however, it has to be said and faced that that NOW is constantly under attack and is considerably hampered by the inroads of flesh, world and devil. The sinful world is not conducive to Christian living – and is not always tolerant of it either. Thus, even as Paul writes to Philippi, he is himself in prison *because* of his Christian activity, and he senses that he may well be liquidated. How significant it is that he writes:

'For it has been granted to you on behalf of Christ not only to believe on him, but also to suffer for him, since you are going through the same struggle you saw I had, and now hear that I still have' (1.29–30).

The Philippian church is under attack from outside, as phrases such as 'those who oppose you' (1.28), 'those dogs, those men who do evil' (3.2) and 'enemies of the Cross of Christ' (3.18) reveal. The enemy is, however, also at work *within* the Christian community. Paul reports sadly:

'some preach Christ out of envy and rivalry' and 'selfish ambition' (1.15, 17),

and:

'everyone looks out for his own interests, not those of Jesus Christ' (2.21).

Furthermore, within the little fellowship in Philippi, there is a break of fellowship between two of the foremost women (4.2). So the NOW in Christ is hampered; it is incomplete and imperfect, for

> 'we do *not yet* see everything in subjection to Jesus Christ' (Hebrews 2.8.RSV).

Thirdly, the NOT YET awaits Christ's men and women, and it will be utterly splendid. Yes, Paul writes 'for to me, to live is Christ . . .' and he means each syllable, but he adds, and equally means, 'and to die is gain' (1.21); and again, 'to depart and be with Christ . . . is better by far (1.23). Paul's Christian confidence is that the NOW needs and leads into the far greater NOT YET:

> 'I want to know Christ and the power of his resurrection and the fellowship of sharing in his sufferings, becoming like him in his death, and so, somehow, to attain to the resurrection from the dead. Not that I have already obtained all this, or have already been made perfect, but I press on to take hold of that for which Christ Jesus took hold of me. Brothers, I do not consider myself yet to have taken hold of it. But one thing I do: Forgetting what is behind and straining towards what is ahead, I press on towards the goal to win the prize for which God has called me heavenwards in Christ Jesus' (3.10–14).

Paul reminds the Philippians of the glorious NOT YET which awaits them and him together:

> 'But our citizenship is in heaven. And we eagerly await a Saviour from there, the Lord Jesus Christ, who, by the power that enables him to bring everything under his control, will transform our lowly bodies so that they will be like his glorious body' (3.20–21).

The very next verse

> 'therefore, my brothers, . . . that is how you should stand firm in the Lord' (4.1)

shows how the greater NOT YET fortifies the NOW which is great but attacked and often frustrated.

Holding the 'now' and the 'not yet' together

Our Christian expectations, then, must take account of both the 'now' and the 'not yet' of Christian experience. As the Holy Spirit flows in a radically renewing way, the 'now' of the Christian's experience is rescued from dullness and lethargy: a wonderfully new immediacy and intimacy irradiates his relationship with God, and a wonderfully new power his discipleship. He wants to share what he himself has been graciously given: he wants others to know, enjoy and thrive upon the rich resources of Christ available *'now'* for newness of being. I want to say a resounding 'YES!' to all of that – and to add that we may nevertheless not legitimately expect *all* of heaven here and now. What we are offered now is, as a chef might put it, a 'soupçon', a real but tiny taste. This is what Paul is expressing when he characterizes our direct personal experiencing of the Spirit as the 'arrhabon':

> 'God put His Spirit in our hearts as a "arrhabon", guaranteeing what is to come' (2 Corinthians 1.22).

'Arrhabon' is a first instalment which guarantees the rest. We may expect *'now'* a first instalment, a down payment, a secure deposit, of all that is ours in Christ, but we may *not* expect the whole: the whole, the full glory, is yet to come. The authentic Christian message concerning the here and now, therefore, is neither perfectionism nor triumphalism; we counsellors have no biblical (or experiential) warrant to lead counselees to suppose that their lives can be all heaven and all victory right now. The whole creation groans in its subjection to frustration and in its bondage to decay, and looks for the Day of the glorious freedom of the children of God. Meanwhile, we who have the *'firstfruits'* of the Spirit, we groan too, as we await that Day: it is not yet (Romans 8.18–23). A Christian is simply not going to be entirely free of difficulties in this life: he is walking the way of the Cross which involves sufferings; tremendous resources are available to him as to his Lord in the days of His flesh, and to be in Christ is the most marvellous place to be, but there are dark days and stiff climbs to endure before the Day. If, in giving counsel, we are teaching or even *seeming* to imply that a counselee can be totally free of emotional, mental or spiritual anguish, then we are doing violence to the revelation of God in Christ and in the New Testament church, and we shall be guilty of doing violence *to our counselee*, for he or she will never attain such a condition before eternity begins.

The footballing world yields an analogy that greatly helps me to keep the '*now*' and the '*not yet*' in a proper perspective. If you listen to football commentators, you will often hear them refer to a player on the field as one who is reckoned to be 'carrying an injury'. The phrase means that that player is not completely fit: he is restricted by a niggle in a groin, a twinge in a knee, a soreness in a tendon. He is in the team because he is needed and is still able to make a genuine contribution to the overall performance of the team. However, he must not expect to do everything perfectly: he must play within the parameters set by his injury, and he must play as one of the *team*. Many of us were injured *before* the game of adult life began, and before we knew ourselves to be chosen for Christ's team, the church. As examples, think of those who have inherited particular characteristics such as extreme shyness; or those who, as little children, were brutalized or sexually abused within their own family circle; or those who were always being pressurized by parents to succeed, but never made the mark; or those born with some physical or mental disadvantage: they all 'bear the marks', and, to some extent, always will. Others of us are injured along the way: circumstances, events, and/or people wound us. If we yield such hurts to our Lord, His healing is substantial – but not total: perhaps we do not allow it to be total, perhaps being part and parcel of sinful humanity it cannot (yet) be total. Just as I carry a physical injury – a weakened muscle in the lower back which signals loud and clear if I am over reaching the limits it sets me – so surely I carry some old war-wounds and sensitivities out of over 25 years of being a pastor! The treasure is in 'jars of clay' (2 Corinthians 4.7): I am one of those jars – and you are another! By this world's measuring, many of us would never be considered, let alone chosen, for the first team! However, as we saw in chapter 1 from our reading of His ministry, Jesus Christ has a special predilection for the disadvantaged. God is like that: He calls the most unlikely of folk to be in His team. Indeed, the rather tart saying currently in vogue, 'if you find the perfect local church, please don't join it – you'll only spoil it!', has its point, for we are none of us whole by the Christ measurement, nor shall we be this side of heaven, nor should we expect to be. On the other hand, our King is '*Abba*', Father, even Daddy, Who cares for His children, Who gives good things to them, Who addresses their needs, Who releases their potential, Who encourages them to grow. Furthermore, it is certainly not for us to impose our limits upon what our God may choose to do to signal the deeper breaking in of His Sovereignty of grace and righteousness on earth. Accordingly, all of us who are in Christ, counsellors and counselees alike, can rightfully be looking to *grow towards* that wholeness and holiness of which the fulness of Christ is the measure. Within limits set by any injuries we carry, we will expect to be increasingly effective members of Christ's Team.

Counsellors must wrestle within themselves to maintain balance between the 'now' and the 'not yet', particularly because the Holy Spirit is lifting flagging Christians into a new level of expectancy, and is bringing to birth many new Christians with a high expectancy of God. We are, praise God! discovering the reality of that rich '*now*' which, if we will receive it, we are graciously given because we are Christ's. That said and rejoiced in, there are ominous signs that the pendulum may swing way beyond the mark set by the New Testament and the Spirit of God – witness the Christian who told me in all seriousness that, subsequent to his 'resting in the Spirit' at a big meeting, he was never again going to have any problems physical, emotional, intellectual, whatever. That position, which some seem to preach, gives people a one-way ticket to self-deception and/or sheer disillusionment. It is phoney. It cannot be substantiated from the whole sweep of either Scripture or life. Church leaders and counsellors have the responsibility to encourage members and counselees firstly, to be filled and to go on being filled with the Spirit; secondly, as William Carey expressed it, to 'expect great things from God, and attempt great things for God'; and thirdly, to accept positively *both* what God gives and does, *and* what (at least to our perception) God does not (yet) give and do. To maintain such a stance is no easy matter, for we are under constant pressure to settle for the simplistic, ostensibly so that all may understand, and the unsure may become sure; and we are equally under pressure to urge those in our charge to expect *everything* now from the hand of God. Planting one foot firmly in the bedrock of biblical testimony, and the other in actual experience of following the Way of Christ here and now, we must refuse to succumb to such pressures or temptations: at the same time, though, we must gladly bear witness that it *is* God's heart to give Christians and counselees a rich expectancy of His continuing grace. We must beware of a 'Rambo' Christianity wherein a rampant Lord obliterates every obstacle to happiness: Jesus eschewed that way (see Matthew 26.53) and continued along the greater Way of the Cross. If our 'renewal' or 'restoration' expectations are unrealistic, dogmatic, man-made rather than Scripture-founded and Spirit-directed, then this Awakening's epitaph may be Haggai 1.9:

'You expected much, but see, it turned out to be little'.

The Lord God spoke that through His prophet just because the People of God had moved out of line with the Word of God and were failing to keep in step with His Spirit.

The matter of personal culpability

In his very helpful manual of caring, *A Friend in Need*, Selwyn Hughes quotes a song by Anna Russell:

I went to my psychiatrist
To be psychoanalysed
To find out why I killed the cat
And blackened my wife's eyes.

He put me on a downy couch
To see what he could find
And this is what he dredged up
From my unconscious mind.

When I was one, my mummy hid

My dolly in the trunk
And so it follows naturally
That I am always drunk.

When I was two, I saw my father
Kiss the maid one day
And that is why I suffer now –
Kleptomania

When I was three, I suffered from
Ambivalence towards my brothers,
So it follows naturally,
I poisoned all my lovers.

I'm so glad that I have learned
The lesson it has taught,
That everything I do that's wrong
Is someone else's fault.

This clever caricature serves to wake us up to the fact that Christians moving freely through counselling books, conferences and courses need to recognize that the doctrine of sin is being subjected to outright attack. Whatever a counselee presents, be it an emotional, intellectual, volitional or behavioural disorder, it appears that there is always an explanation which releases him from being responsible and from being held responsible for how he is and what he is doing. It is somebody else's fault. Blaming 'them' is one of the favourite pastimes of our society in any case: if 'they' had not done this, or had done that, then, of course, I would not have done the other, so 'they' must shoulder the responsibility for what I have done. It is essential that Christian carers and counsellors are clear-eyed concerning this matter of culpability. There are three truths to be held together:

> first, *that the root of many people's current difficulties is somebody else's real or apparent failings or failures*: parental neglect or violence, for example, can have dire consequences for the offspring – in that sense, and in that sense only, the Hebrew proverb 'the fathers eat sour grapes, and the children's teeth are set on edge' has its point;

> second, *that they themselves are responsible for the way they choose*

37

to continue to react to what happened to them: this is a hard saying but so important, for wounded people will not find healing until they cease to blame others for how they now are, until they acknowledge that although they did not choose what happened to them, they *do* choose how to continue to feel, think and act;

third, *that some of their reactions are sinful which makes them themselves personally culpable before God*: hating, brooding over thoughts of vengeance, verbal character-assassination and the whole catalogue of like reactions are sin, and lock the sinners into solidarity with the very sinners they are blaming.

What we counsellors must needs do is make that journey of threefold understanding, coming to terms with each truth. It is here that the gospel of Jesus Christ comes into its own, for it is only the power of the Cross that can break the stranglehold of sin and its consequences, by bringing us to repentance, by enabling us to experience the cleansing and liberating energy of forgiveness, and by releasing into us the resources of the Holy Spirit whereby we can forgive others and ourselves. In understanding people's needs and then in counselling them, let us never be ashamed of the Truth which Jesus Christ is, even though initially it may be extremely painful for counselees to respond to His loving of them or His call for them to love, for one of the major afflictions besetting humankind and keeping men and women in bondage to destructive reactions is defiant unforgivingness – and another is unforgivenness. In this crucial area, the Christian counsellor more than any other has good news to bring and a new way of being to depict. The Christian doctrine of culpability before God being met with salvation and forgiveness through Jesus Christ is not outmoded: rather, secularization has carelessly pushed it aside, for which act we are now paying a terrible price in the rising numbers of those who cannot and will not cope with their unchecked destructive reactions. The truth is plain: most of all, they need to acknowledge their own responsibility and culpability before God, and thus their need of a Saviour and a Lord, to come to Christ, and to live differently in the power of His Spirit.

3

Where is your own reliance?

For many of my formative years, my family occupied a rather old three-storey house in Handsworth, part of inner-city Birmingham. There were drawbacks about that old place (for example, it actually shifted on its foundations in a high wind) but one distinct advantage was that we all had plenty of space. Between my elder brother's room and mine, there was a box-room, quite large, and christened by us 'the glory-hole'! In it we stored anything that was not actually in current use, so that over the years it acquired such a huge accumulation of all sorts that for us lads, climbing into it became an adventure in itself!

To my mind, that is how the Spirit of God finds us when he freshly draws near by the grace of God, insisting upon entrance in the Name of Jesus Christ. When the Spirit of God comes in renewal, He does not encounter a vacuum, but a veritable storehouse of things, a huge and tangled accumulation out of the years consisting of things good, bad and indifferent. He then sets about that difficult sifting process of keeping for restoration and use, what is good, but also, painfully, of throwing out what is not. In respect of pastoral care and counselling, when the Spirit comes, we already have in that department an accumulation of ideas, assumptions, habits, perhaps convictions, perhaps techniques and expertise, certainly experiences. We are a box-room of counselling (and other) all-sorts! So what to do as, by the Spirit, the living Lord raps upon our door? He is the *'Wonderful Counsellor'*. We can but open up the whole room to Him, give Him entrance, give Him permission to investigate all that is in there. Christian counsellors need *His counsel*. Our box-room of preconceptions may be deep and cluttered: it takes time for everything in there to·be uncovered, evaluated and then dealt with, so it is crucial that we *remain* open to Him. What might be there in our box-room?

a) What we have picked up and stored away from secular counselling
There are now so many books about methods of counselling, and so many counselling courses and conferences available to Christian workers. Most of the books, courses and conferences, however, draw upon the behavioural sciences in general and secular counselling therapies in particular, to a greater or lesser extent. Whereas I shall argue in chapter 5, that there is a great deal for us to garner from secular counselling practitioners and schools of therapy, I am now pointing out that those of us who have sought to study something of the bewildering range of theories and techniques in regard to actual counselling, secular or Christian, may well, all unwittingly, have imbibed presuppositions which are something less than Christian. Personally, I find it hard to countenance that any Christian could feel comfortable with the bleak behaviourism of a Skinner or the arid determinism of a Freud. However, I would surely not be alone in Christian circles if I say that I have, for example, tried to sharpen my skills by opening my mind and ministry to the considerable waves caused by the writings of Carl Rogers, and by those who have built upon his findings. Rogerian counselling makes us take seriously the *nature of the relationship* between counsellor and counselee, insisting that, however knowledgeable he may be, if the counsellor is not able or willing to build an *authentic relationship* with his counselee, then not only may he well not help the counselee, he may actually leave him more damaged than when the counselling began. When the Rogerian school calls for *person-centred* counselling, for a counselling relationship which *itself encourages personal growth*, and which is characterized by the Rogerian triad of *accurate empathy, non-possessive warmth, and genuineness* there is so much there which instinctively appeals to the Christian carer. It would not be at all difficult to illustrate such qualities of caring relationship by direct reference to the ministry of Jesus. I believe that I have

benefitted considerably by being thus persuaded to examine the *nature* of the counselling relationship itself. However, there is a snag: at the end of the day, Rogerian perspectives and presuppositions are frankly humanist and agnostic. Secular psychotherapy is pervaded with the modern 'do-it-yourself' syndrome: the achieving of progress or goals depends upon man's own resources; what most matters is a person's own satisfaction within a generally accepted social framework. It is a system of self-help. The underlying orientation is always *self* orientation. There is no sin; there is no God; there is no Christ crucified and risen for us and for our salvation; there is no new life in Christ, with Christ and for Christ. Accordingly, if we have read counselling books and attended counselling courses, it is particularly important that we keep our own counselling box-room open for inspection by the Spirit of Christ.

b) What we have picked up and stored away from our own church tradition
Being the Pastor of a denominational local church which has been profoundly searched by 'charismatic renewal', I never cease to be both amazed and perturbed by the tenacity of 'tradition'. I do not despise the Christian 'tradition' – indeed, I value it greatly insofar as it stands guard over the deposit of what has been handed down to us of Christ and His Truth. What I ask, however, is whether much of what is fiercely defended as our tradition is in fact Christian at all? What disturbs me most is that the arguments engendered by the blowing of the Spirit into a local church seem hardly ever to be based upon Scripture. Some arguments are transparently untenable, and yet doggedly stuck to: I am told, for example, that for some church members, only old hymns (i.e. those in that church's hymn-book) are accepted as being 'hymns', so that new compositions (Graham Kendrick's superb 'Meekness and Majesty', for example) which are manifestly hymns, are rejected and, by the stubborn few, not sung at all for that reason! What Scriptural or Christian principle is in play here, I ask myself? I reluctantly conclude from my years in the pastoral ministry that the true 'tradition' has become encrusted with accretions which are of the flesh and of the world – and can even become demonically infested. So, in

regard to the ministry of counselling care, what might your tradition have bequeathed to you as its legacy?

It is only relatively recently that I have found myself moving in circles which are firmly labelled 'evangelical'. In terms of commitment to the Lord, of the desire to worship, to explore the Bible and to serve and witness to the Lord, and of wanting to hear and to obey His Word, it is proving to be thrilling company. Yet, having arrived by a different route, I can perhaps in some small measure view the evangelical scene without evangelical spectacles. The particular dangers of its tradition, I sense, remain those of bibliolatry, anti-intellectualism and a certain unwillingness to be exposed to other points of view. Translated into counselling terms, that can work out at a dark suspicion of all psychology, psychiatry and psychotherapy, and a consequent reluctance to acquire those skills and understandings which the secular therapies show to be essential for effective counselling communications. A further consequence can be a method of counselling which assumes that all that is required is (a) to find the problem, then (b) to find a Scripture which applies to it, and (c) to hit the former with the latter. Yes, I am caricaturing somewhat to make my point – which is that any such attitude on the part of a counsellor could prove destructive to a counselee, Christian or not, who is suffering from a deeply embedded emotional/mental neurosis. It is not Scripture of itself that heals. It is God who heals, and He heals by moving into real relationship with us: to Him, we are each not a 'problem', but a very precious individual. In our attitude towards, and our use of, Scripture in counselling, it behoves us to heed the warnings of Paul concerning the antithesis of 'the letter' and 'the Spirit':

Romans 2.29:	'Circumcision is circumcision of the heart, by the Spirit, not by the written code' (the letter).
Romans 7.6:	'But now, by dying to what once bound us, we have been released from the law so that we serve in the new way of the Spirit, and not in the old way of the written code' (the letter).

2 Corinthians 3.5–6:   'We are not competent in ourselves to claim anything for ourselves, but our competence comes from God. He has made us competent as ministers of a new covenant – not of the letter but of the Spirit; *for the letter kills, but the Spirit gives life.*'

We need to check frequently that our usage of Scripture, supposedly to liberate people, has not degenerated into the mode of 'the letter' which weighs them down. It is a real question then: what has our particular church tradition actually deposited in our counselling box-room?

c) What we have picked up and stored away from our surrounding society

We may not have become particularly acquainted with Rogerian or any other counselling emphases and styles, nor may we have been the child of any particularly emphatic church tradition: however, none of us can possibly escape being a part of the society which surrounds us, which means that we need to come to terms sensibly with the reality that the whole ethos of our society is secular. There is an all-pervading God-ignoring scientism in the very atmosphere of our society, and we all breathe it in. The consequent acid rains of secularism, materialism, consumerism and hedonism, all of which really presuppose that 'this is all there is', are constantly falling upon our Christian foliage. What they do, in effect, is to deny any reality to the spiritual and the supernatural – or, at very least, relegate them to the periphery of life. If there is anything in them (and if there is, it will soon be analysed and rationally mastered), it is certainly not central; they are significant for neither the understanding nor the living of life. Man is the master of things – and has to be, for there is none other to take the role. This is a bleak philosophy. It has the effect, though, of making belief in the supernatural seem the province of 'cranks', so that any person who, with vigour, puts credence in God is regarded as 'off-centre', someone definitely to be steered clear of. I believe that this arid philosophy (which holds millions in thrall without their knowing it) can have a corrosive effect upon unprotected Christian commitment and vitality. After all, at least two people in three in this nation apparently claim a belief in the Christian God, yet for the majority of those, it remains a belief that plainly has no substance since it makes not a whit of difference to their lives. Its vigour, its relevance, has been corroded. Its arms and legs have withered and dropped off.

When I was a youngster, I developed an abiding love for butterflies. I took to breeding them right through the cycle from egg to adult butterfly. It is an amazing cycle, and particularly, of course, the metamorphosis of caterpillar to butterfly, through the 'death' of pupation (the chrysalis stage). Naturally and inevitably, it has become vivid imagery for encapsulating the central Christian affirmation about being 'born again' into newness of life. My particular perception is that too many of us born again Christian butterflies remain, or allow ourselves again to become, earth-bound. We do not fly. We are not flying. We have retained or re-acquired the earth-bound mind-set of the caterpillar. We have absorbed unknowingly the agnostic rationalism of our environment which says that earth-bound caterpillars we are, so, Christian variety or not, we can only crawl along in a manner appropriate to caterpillars. Yet we Christians are born again from *above* in Christ, we have the wings of the Spirit, and are commissioned to be new-life butterflies; we are called to lift off into the spiritual *above*, into the supernatural, and to soar into more and more of the vastness of the Way, the Truth and the Life which Christ Jesus is; is *always*; is *now*. As the Holy Spirit renews the People of God, so many Christians are being released to fly (again). As the Word says:

'But those who hope in the Lord will renew their strength. They will *soar on wings* like eagles' (Isaiah 40.31).

We need to find out whether we have stored in our box-room societal presuppositions which would keep us and our counselling care earth-bound.

O Lord,
Let the morning bring me word of Your unfailing love,
for I have put my trust in You. Show me the way I should
Go. . . . (Psalm 143.8).

I have to acknowledge that when the searchlight of the
Spirit and the Word flooded my counselling ministry with
light, what was revealed was essentially a man-reliant
ministry. The counselee was relying upon *me* to give help
and effect change; I was relying, firstly, upon *myself* to be
empathetic, to uncover the problem, to draw upon my knowledge and experience, to feed in relevant Bible passages and
Christian guidelines, and thus to give good counsel; and,
secondly, upon the *counselee* to think through, pray in and act
upon the wisdom I had imparted. I am not denying the place
and the validity of such processes of counselling; rather, I am
wanting to point out that the immediate God and His power
actually play no living part in such a counselling scenario.
Neither the counselee nor I is looking to the Lord; we are not
expecting Him to have any direct input – and, therefore, at
bottom, our reliance is upon ourselves. When, however, the
Holy Spirit takes possession of our counselling box-room, He
Himself takes up, gives His life to, and uses, our listening
skills, our empathizing, our ability to discern, make connections and see the shape of deep-down difficulties, our acquired
wisdom and our experience, our knowledge of the Scriptures
and our grasp of Christian truth: He in no way cancels out
who I am (or who the counselee is), but the Lord is vastly
more able than we are or can ever be. He has tremendous
resources for our counselling, as for every area of our discipleship, resources which are available through Christ and by
the Spirit. It is of the very essence of renewal that Christians
are brought alive (again) to the reality that the Spirit is able
daily, hourly, to bring power-filled resources to us from the
Father and the Son. The reinstatement of the Person and the
Power of the Holy Spirit to a rightful place vis-à-vis the
church and her ministries means that we can have real access
to the intentions and the resources of the Father and the Son,
as we seek to counsel. That being so, our base position for
all counselling enterprises needs to be: 'in You, O Lord, do
I put my trust'. For authentically Christian counselling, we

45

need Christ in the Spirit to be to the fore of our ministerings, to keep us in direct contact with the mind and heart of God.

'Go on being filled with the spirit. . . .'

As we know, that is the force of Ephesians 5.18. Not only do we need the Spirit of Christ to come to the fore of our ministering, we need Him to *continue* to be there.

A Bible passage I am drawn to is John 1.32–34:

> 'Then John gave this testimony: "I saw the Spirit come down from heaven as a dove and remain on Him. I would not have known Him, except that the One Who told me to baptize with water told me 'The man on whom you see the Spirit come down and remain is He Who will baptize with the Holy Spirit'. I have seen and I testify that this is the Son of God".'

My sense is that the words '*and remain*' are theologically rich: the implication has to be that the fullness of the Holy Spirit is always upon Jesus of Nazareth, i.e. is not always upon anyone else. A part of the uniqueness, an aspect of the divinity of Jesus, is that the fullness of the Spirit is always upon, with and in Him, whereas with the rest of men, it is not so.

In this connection, another Gospels passage I am drawn to is that where the disciples of Jesus embarrassingly fail to expel an unclean spirit which was incapacitating a young lad. The episode is recounted by Mark (9.14–29) being retold by both Matthew (17.14–21) and Luke (9.37–43). The really intriguing thing about this failure is that it occurs *after* Jesus had given His men His authority and power so that they themselves could preach the Good News of the Kingdom breaking in, and could themselves initiate the Kingdom 'signs' of healing the sick and casting out alien spirits. All the indications are that initially they did just that, including dealing with demons or evil spirits:

> 'They went out and preached that people should repent. *They drove out many demons* and anointed many sick people with oil and healed them' (Mark 6.12–13).

That being so, how come that nine of the twelve together could not shift an evil spirit in a young lad? Jesus makes it clear that the obstruction is not in the boy or his father – the obstacle is 'unbelief' and includes the disciples themselves. When they enquire of Jesus why He is able to expel the demon when they had said and done the same as He, Jesus replies, Mark 9.29: 'This kind can come out only by prayer'. What that surely indicates is that somehow the disciples have shifted away from direct reliance upon the Lord's power: they said the right words, but nothing happened. It is so easy to become blasé about ministry – and then, somehow, the power of the Spirit ceases to flow. I would suspect that that corresponds with the experience of many for whom spiritual renewal was initially so profoundly empowering. The power of the Holy Spirit is no automatic possession, and there are times both for local churches and for individual disciples when the immediacy and the power are no longer there; in one way or another, the church or the disciple has slipped out of being directly dependent upon the sovereign grace of God.

Paul perceived that something of that nature had occurred within the Galatian churches:

> 'Are you so foolish? After beginning with the Spirit, are you now trying to attain your goal by human effort?' (Galatians 3.3).

They had begun by trusting the Lord directly – and yet had now shifted out of faith and back into a religion of works from the burden of which Christ had set them free! Such shifting still happens in twentieth-century churches.

During the 20 years I have so far been the pastor of Brickhill Baptist Church in Bedford, some 60 men and women who gladly confessed Jesus Christ as Saviour and Lord, and were welcomed into church membership, have 'lapsed'. Insofar as we are able to assess, their Christian commitment has collapsed, and they appear now to have no Christian confession to make. What happened? There may, of course, have been faults and failings on our part as their local church, but the Lord did not fail them or forsake them, did He? No, critically, they ceased to walk with Him, ceased to maintain live communion with Him, and, by one route or another, ended up in the kind of life-without-God from which Jesus Christ had once delivered them. They *began* with the Spirit: *but they did not continue.*

I am convinced that the major issue confronting the current (or any) profound renewal and restoration movement is that of *sustaining* it: that issue needs to be placed squarely on the Christian agenda *now*. It needs to be on the agenda of us Christian carers and counsellors too, lest we also fall back into trying to obtain our goals by human effort. Accordingly, we need to address the vital issue of the *constant* renewing of our dependence upon God; to that end, however, let us first be sure that we recognize the *process* by which we ourselves or counselees can be seduced away from living reliance upon the Spirit of God.

a) The sabotage process

It is quite clear from a reading of Galatians that there were those who were actively seeking to undermine the Gospel of Grace which Paul had preached, which the Galatian Christians had believed, and which the Spirit of the Sovereign Lord had confirmed with gifts and signs. Indeed, the Book of Acts shows us that Paul's missionary journeys were dogged by opponents intent upon wrecking his meetings and his mission-ministry. The record of the Gospels similarly demonstrates that the ministry of Jesus was subject to deliberate harassment. In both cases, the opponents were intentionally inseminating the minds of would-be disciples with accusations, insinuations and horror-stories, so as to sabotage the ministries of Jesus and Paul. One of the saddest verses in the Gospels must surely be John 6.66: 'From this time, many of his disciples turned back and no longer followed Him'. Although, in the Johannine context, it is 'hard teaching' which offends and causes them to fall away, there can be little doubt but that the sabotaging tactics of the opposition did bear fruit. There are those in our scene today who oppose our work. Some would-be disciples who have fallen by the wayside have done so essentially because they were 'nobbled' – adversely influenced by the anti or the aggrieved. Probably we Christians have become too 'nice': when people do attack by smear, perhaps we should exhibit a bit more of the robustness of the Apostle who writes openly:

'As for those agitators, I wish they would go the whole way and emasculate themselves!' (Galatians 5.12).

Or a bit more of the explicit frankness of his Lord and ours:

'Woe to you . . . you hypocrites! You are like whitewashed tombs which look beautiful on the outside but on the inside are full of dead men's bones and everything unclean. In the same way, on the outside you appear to people as righteous but on the inside you are full of hypocrisy and wickedness' (Matthew 23.27–28).

Perhaps there is a speaking out which we need to recover in order to protect the flock of God.

b) *The power of reversion*
After his denials and the crucifixion of his Lord, Peter, we are told, went back to fishing, that is, back to whence he had come, back to what had been before Jesus invaded his life. It is reported of a group of prisoners who, remarkably, survived incarceration in the concentration camp at Belsen, that when the Allies liberated the camp, this group of ghostly, emaciated figures walked very slowly out of the gates, paused, blinked, looked around at the free world outside the perimeter fence, and then, wordlessly, turned around as one and shuffled back into Belsen. That is an extreme situation with an extreme psychology, but it does serve to illustrate graphically the pull of the past ways, of the familiar, of the safe, the pull *back* to where we were at home before. At the time when Paul wrote to the Galatian Christians, they are clearly already on their way *back* into the religion of works from which the grace of Christ had liberated them. Made uncertain and confused by teaching contrary to what they had received, they were retreating back into the cocoon the Spirit had coaxed them out of. It may not have been the greatest of places to be, it may not have been the greatest of cocoons as cocoons go, but they *knew* it: it gave them bearings again, and the security of the familiar. In many ways, the whole story of the Old Testa-

ment People of God can stand as a further warning to us to be on guard against the power of 'reversion' (the word means returning to a previous state or habit). Over and over, in the tale of the Judges, in the record of the Kings, in the oracles of the Prophets, it is crystal-clear that a renewal of faith is too often and too soon followed by a turning away which is also a turning back. The crisis over and the need for renewal past, the People lapse back into carelessness, complacency and worse. '*Again* the Israelites did evil in the eyes of the Lord' is a depressingly recurrent refrain. Mercifully, it is balanced by the hopeful cry of the Lord:

'Even now', declares the Lord, 'return to me with all your heart . . .
Rend your heart and not your garments.
Return to the Lord your God, for he is gracious and compassionate . . .' (Joel 2.12–13).

Let us see the danger of reversion ourselves, and draw others' attention to it. May the many to whom the Lord has given a whole new lease of life for the work of the Kingdom not be pulled away and drawn back to former ways where He is by no means Lord. The Parable of the Sower (Mark 4.1–9) bears eloquent testimony that Jesus Himself fervently echoes that prayer.

c) The power of erosion
Many more of us Christians do not lapse as such. Our commitment to Christ is real and tenacious, and we have a dogged attachment to His Church, too, for all its imperfections, and whatever betide. What happens spiritually when our relationship with God is not being truly renewed and refreshed, however, is that we lose the immediacy of His Presence and the flow of His Power. Our spiritual vitality and alertness are *eroded*. A certain joylessness and inertia creep in, and we move (sometimes almost imperceptibly) over into habit. Our discipleship and our church-involvements are now boosted only by sporadic attempts at fervent prayer, plus sundry other efforts on our part to gee ourselves up. One of the most powerful agents of spiritual erosion, especially for Christian leaders and others deeply involved in the Lord's

work, is *familiarity* or, indeed, *over-familiarity* – in this sense, that a new freedom in worship is no longer 'new' as the years pass; the new song is not 'new' once you have sung it twenty times; and new gifts of the Spirit are not 'new' as experience mounts. They are all as Christianly *valid* as ever, but they are not *new* in the way they first were. I am *not* advocating a ceaseless search for the excitingly new and different (that is a road to superficiality) but I am underpinning every way I can the primary importance of constant spiritual renewing. Otherwise, we shall belong to a people whose arms are lifted high whilst their hearts are nowhere in particular, and a people who sing without their minds. We should surely take note that one of the Old Testament verses which Jesus chose to highlight is Isaiah 29.13:

'These people come near to me with their mouth and honour me with their lips, but their hearts are far from me' (See Matthew 15.8 and Mark 7.6).

We in our day need to beware lest, in our Christian activities such as counselling, we are doing little else than going through the motions of spirituality, making· the noises which we have learned are appropriate. It is with real point and purpose that Paul urges the Galatians:

'Live by the Spirit', literally '*walk*' by the Spirit (5.16) and more,
'keep in step with the Spirit' (5.25).

Saints alive!

The sustaining of spirituality is crucial. The key is one which we all know only too well. It is that of spending unhindered and unhurried quality time in the presence of God. It is giving the Scriptures room and space to leap across to us as living Word from God. It is giving the Spirit unpressurized opportunity to pray within us and to bring the riches of Christ into our very being. Alas! so many of us leaders and committed church-members and counsellors fail to find the time, such is our (Christian) *busyness*. That, I believe, is precisely why Gordon MacDonald's book *Ordering Your Private World* had such a considerable impact: it touched an already raw nerve – we recognized ourselves in his descriptions of how we should *not* be! I vouchsafe that thousands of new resolutions to crack the busyness syndrome were made, to enable first things to come first in our lives and our days, to release quality time to be with God ... and I vouchsafe with equal confidence that most of those resolutions promptly bit the dust in the very busyness they were supposed to resolve. The only church activists I know who have that book but have not found it acutely challenging are those who, to date, have been too busy to find the time to read it! I attended a MARC Europe Conference for full-time Church leaders at which over a hundred of us were told that we should not work long hours day after day (because if we do, our effectiveness diminishes – and all counsellors please note!) and that one half of the hours we do work should be given to the 'work' of being with God. Even though that time was allowed to include sermon preparation, I can still hear the audible gasp which arose from a totally incredulous audience! Yet, if we leaders are not finding good time to spend in the presence of God, what is going to happen to our churches? and, specifically for our present purposes, to our Christian counselling?

At another gathering of church leaders, I 'chanced' to hear the story of a local church which, after some years of renewal experience, had somehow lost its zeal: the pursuance of its mission-ministry seemed now to be akin to walking through treacle! Eventually, a Day of Prayer was called, and *the* fruit of that occasion was one of those so-simple-but-piercing picture-Words: one of the folk as she prayed 'saw' Jesus sitting on a river-bank all alone and sad because His People were all so busy with their schemes and problems that they had no time or inclination to go to the river-bank to be still with Him, just *being* with Him. The words attached to the picture were simply: 'Tell My People'. So she did. What she reported had a profound impact upon all who heard to the extent that a new lease of life was inaugurated for that fellowship as they began to go to the river-bank. However, as I heard this story relayed, it hit *me* with great force, and I knew that this was also living Word to me and the fellowship I belong to: so I took it back and reported, and we were stirred to repent and to go to the river-bank, with the result that there has been a new zest and sureness in respect of who we are in Christ and what He would have us do for Him. There is no substitute for spending quality time with Him, and it may well be that the river-bank Word is for many more churches yet.

If those of us who are called to and involved with counselling are going to be effective servants of the Lord's purposes for people, we need to be in the flow of living relationship with Him so that He is the senior partner and prime mover in our whole counselling ministry. That way, we may enable those whom we are counselling to establish live connection between themselves with their difficulties and the living, loving Lord with His resources to meet their needs, and to draw them on towards their wholeness. If we and they allow the Spirit day by day to lead us afresh into live connection with and reliance upon the Lord, then, indeed, we shall find

'His compassions never fail: they are new every morning' (Lamentations 3.22–23).

To experience that, day by day, is of the essence for all Christian carers, counsellors and counselees.

KEY RESOURCES

4

Our local church community

'Just as each of us has one body with many members, and
these members do not all have the same function, so in
Christ we who are many form one body, and each member
belongs to all the others' (Romans 12.4–5).

The major resource for Christian care and counselling is the
local Christian community itself; it is the Body of Christ, and
Christ cares, counsels and heals through it. I am convinced
that this dimension of the community of the Church being
itself therapeutic is not yet believed or presented nearly
enough. Certainly the inflow of the Spirit of Christ has given
renewed vigour to the church as the Body of Christ and as
the Family of God, both *community* figures of speech; church
leaders need to continue to put emphasis there because
members live in a society which advocates self sufficiency and
self advancement, applauding individual 'success'. Most talk
of 'community' is mere rhetoric; in most areas, now even
rural ones, the 'community' has little reality beyond that of
a geographical designation. In the row of houses where I live,
garden fences are rather deliberately 6ft high, the intention
being 'privacy' not 'community'. In my area, as in so many,
there are only little pockets of community, focal points being
the school, the pub, the allotments and the church. The
church today is giving the 'Body' and the 'Family' imagery
high profile, encouraging people both to belong and to
discover their function in the whole, but perhaps the
pendulum has swung too much towards an emphasis upon

responsibility (many membership covenants stress the responsibility of membership) and away from privilege. At any given point in time, there are members who need to receive the therapeutic *benefits* of belonging. Ideally that should simply happen, and sometimes it does; but in practice, we need to remind people, to *connect* them with the healing power of belonging to the community of Christ. There are two important corollaries to this: firstly, that church leaders ensure that the high privileges of Christian community are being made available to the people (it is a well known fact in all walks of life that many people do not know of the benefits which are theirs by right) and secondly, that counsellors are aware of these privileges and of their power to heal, and do not view their counselling work as in any way being separate from the communal life of the Church. So what are the powerful resources present within Christian community itself?

A. The healing power of communal conviction

'For this reason I kneel before the Father, from whom his whole family in heaven and on earth derives its name. I pray that out of his glorious riches he may strengthen you with power through his spirit in your inner being, so that Christ may dwell in your hearts through faith. And I pray that you, being rooted and established in love, may have power together with all the saints, to grasp how wide and long and high and deep is the love of Christ, and to know this love that surpasses knowledge – that you may be filled to the measure of all the fullness of God' (Ephesians 3.14–19).

In the original, all of that is a single sentence, and few sentences could be richer in resources; it manages to embrace something of the grace, the riches, the power and the love of the Father, the Son and the Spirit *and* to stress the importance of grasping and knowing and being rooted and established in those living Gospel realities. The Christian community is secure because it has strong foundations; the community has basic non-negotiable convictions which give it cohesion and strength. Its members need to grasp that, need to know it, need to be rooted and established in such foundational faith. Our fellowship in Bedford has its own membership handbook known as 'The Foundations'. In its present form, the document might not satisfy everyone, and, as the years pass, may cease wholly to satisfy us, but its ministry to us is to remind us of the bedrock of Christian truth. Thus its sections are: The Kingdom of God; the Grace of the King Who is Father; Jesus Christ crucified and risen, Saviour and Lord; the empowering of the Holy Spirit: and the loved, saved and enabled Church of Jesus Christ – supplemented by guidelines for our church family life together, plus a statement of our vision and therefore of our goals as a fellowship of Christ's people. We have certainly not managed to reach a place where every member of our Church community *owns* and is *grasped by* these foundations; however, there can be no doubt as to the solidity and living power they give us as a community. Accordingly, when members are hurting, struggling, sinking, or failing, the communal Christian conviction can be drawn upon and come into play in a powerfully reassuring, healing and uplifting way. Furthermore, in situations where our counsellors become involved, there is a common fund of shared Christian fundamentals to draw upon, these fundamentals being in any case the bedrock of Christian counselling. Christian convictions and experiences are a tremendous resource for people. Jeremiah expresses that in a striking figure of speech: whereas, he says, a person who draws only upon his own fleshly reserves for his strength will be like a scrubby bush in the desert, he who trusts in the Lord and whose confidence is in Him will be like a tree planted by a stream, strong and fruitbearing (Jeremiah 17.5–8). We need to enable our people to put down roots which draw upon the river of life flowing from the throne of God (Revelation 22.1–2), through and out of the Church (Ezekiel 47.1–12).

B. The healing power of communal activity

'Therefore, since we have a great high priest who has gone through the heavens, Jesus the Son of God, let us hold firmly to the faith we profess. For we do not have a high priest who is unable to sympathize with our weaknesses, but we have one who has been tempted in every way, just as we are – yet was without sin. Let us then approach the throne of grace with confidence, so that we may receive mercy and find grace to help us in our time of need' (Hebrews 4.14–16).

Whilst that exhortation may be fulfilled in personal devotion, the Old Testament paradigm is that of corporate worship. The primary communal activity of the People of God is worship, the essence of which is encounter with the God Who loves to heal His children and draw them further along the path to wholeness. Christian counselling needs to point to corporate worship as one of the contexts in which inner turmoil can be resolved because the risen Christ moves among His people by His Spirit as they gather in His name. It is unfortunate when people withdraw from the activity of corporate worship because they are troubled, and we who move alongside them should encourage them to gather with the people, and, with the whole company, to seek to draw near to the throne of grace; our great High Priest is well able to sympathize with our weakness, so we do not need to withdraw from Him on the grounds that our weaknesses have (temporarily) gained the upper hand. The ground of worship is not how we feel, but who He is and what He has done and does do on our behalf.

All the major elements of worship are needed for the all-round health and healing of the church community, and it is essential, therefore, that all these major elements are represented frequently in the worship of the Church. The advantage of set liturgy is that all the moods of worship can be written in, although the danger of lapsing into dull repetition through over-familiarity with the script is fairly considerable. The advantage of charismatic worship is freshness and creative variety, but the disadvantages have to do with a menu which may be deficient in vital areas of worship. What is urgently required at the local church level is agreement as to what the essential elements of worship are, the teaching of those elements to the people, and their exposure to and experience of them in corporate worship. Somewhat alarmed at the imbalance of much charismatic worship (too often, little but triumphant praise occupies the centre stage), I have been driven to re-state the ingredients which make for fully rounded worship over a period of, say, a few weeks, in order to present them to our worship team, insisting that they are worked into our worship. The teaching model I use is one which Leslie Weatherhead first published over 30 years ago in his book *A Private House of Prayer* (Hodder and Stoughton). The book was primarily intended as an aid to private devotion but it also serves to highlight the major themes of corporate worship. Each theme is represented as a room in a house, and, for fully rounded relating with God, there are seven rooms to be visited as follows:

Room 1 is the place where we *affirm the presence of God*. Instead of dashing into the motions or noises of worship, we focus upon the abiding spiritual reality that we are in the presence of God; we recollect·His presence, we encourage our minds, wills, hearts and spirits to gather around that unchanging truth, we allow His Word 'Be still and know that I am God' to register.

Room 2 is the place of *praise, thanksgiving and adoration*. Here we marvel at, rejoice in, respond to the love, the majesty, the power, the glory, the holiness, the wisdom and the grace of our God as Father, Son and Holy Spirit, and we express our thankfulness for all He has been, is, and will be to us. We dwell upon *Him*.

Room 3 is the place of *confession, forgiveness and unloading*. Here we confess our sins of commission and omission, together with the jealousy, the malice, the pride, the intolerance, the impurity, the resentment, the indifference, the deception, the greed and the fear which gave rise to them. We repent of all these not in order to wallow, but to ask for and receive the forgiveness of God: He loves to forgive those who genuinely seek His forgiveness, He loves His children to know that they are loved, cleansed, forgiven and accepted. In this room too, we give over to our Father our confusion, our hurt, our worry, our guilt and shame, all the weights that slow us down in the race for which we are entered.

Room 4 bears the sign *'affirmation and reception'*. This is not the most well known room by a long way, yet it is one which offers a very great deal. To be cleansed and unloaded is one thing, to be filled is quite another, and this is too often our point of failure. So this is the place where we turn from our sinfulness and frailty to the rocksure promises of God, and allow those promises to permeate our inmost being: for example, at the Last Supper, Jesus says to his friends:

'I tell you the truth, anyone who has faith in me will do what I have been doing. He will do even greater things than these, because I am going to the Father. And I will do whatever you ask in my name, so that the Son may bring glory to the Father. You may ask me for anything in my name, and I will do it' (John 14.12–14).

'Peace I leave with you; my peace I give you. I do not give to you as the world gives. Do not let your hearts be troubled and do not be afraid' (John 14.27).

Our heads know those words very well, but our very being needs to be soaked in our Lord's tremendous assurances, so, quietly, unhurriedly, we now receive those promises, we let the Lord speak them to us, and we affirm them for ourselves, we feed on them with faith.

Room 5 is the place set aside for *purified desire and sincere petition*. This is where we continue the discipling process of opening our motives, our ambitions, our dominant desires to the searchlight of our Lord's love, until, perhaps, our truest petition is more akin to that of Kagawa of Japan: 'Make me like Jesus'. We ask Father God to grow within us more of the faith, the hope, the love and the radiance of Jesus.

Room 6 is the room for *intercession for others' good*. There are various ways of doing that, but one particularly helpful to me is an expansion of Leslie Weatherhead's own: let us suppose that we are praying for 'Margaret': the method is to 'see' her as you speak her name to the Lord, to 'see' her and the Lord move together, and to watch her emerging from her difficulties as he ministers to her. I like the comment of George MacDonald: 'I will not say that I will pray for you, but I shall think of God and you together'.

Room 7 is set aside for *unhurried meditation*, in particular, dwelling imaginatively upon a passage of Scripture, so that the Lord may feed us with fresh truth.

When, in this way, one assembles the major elements of worship, it is immediately obvious what a powerful instrument for pastoral care and counselling public worship can be *by its very nature*. When we are turning in upon ourselves, the worship of God's people leads us into rooms where we affirm the presence of God and praise, thank and adore Him, where we intercede for others, and where we meditate upon God's word – all activities which, by taking us out of ourselves, save us from the perils of unhealthy introspection. When we are hating ourselves or other people, the place of confession, forgiveness and unloading, followed by that of affirming and receiving the promises of God, can be the instigation of our healing. When we are hurting, to be taken into rooms filled with God's presence and promises, and into places where we can unload and purify our desires, can keep us from going over into sinful responses and consequent emotional torment. By affording a congregation constant opportunities wherein God cares for the people, gives them good counsel, cleanses, heals, renews and encourages them, corporate worship becomes a front line care and counselling resource. Counsellors need to know that and share it, perceiving that for counselees to be involved in public worship aids and abets the whole counselling process. Church leaders need to understand that one part of their responsibility is to take an overview of the public worship to check that, over a period of weeks, the essential ingredients are all being incorporated.

Praise is very popular, but what about confession? and purifying our desires? and intercession? and meditation? The fresh inflow of the Spirit has caused the People of God to burst anew into song, but how few songs there are like John Wimber's 'Oh Lord, have mercy upon me' which can take a congregation into a place of unloading and confession, and how few like 'Make me a channel of your peace Lord' (and that borrowed from St. Francis of Assisi!) which take us right into 'Make me like Jesus' petition. Moreover, the frequent singing of the same songs of renewal can so easily slide over into that very going-through-the-motions condition from which the Spirit moved in to rescue us: if, however, the songs are being consciously linked with, and presented in the context of a particular 'room' of worship, then their 'life' can be extended, a principle which applies equally to many great hymns of former days. Full-bodied corporate worship reduces counselling queues!

As a postscript in respect of the healing power of communal activity, let it be said that there are effective forms of communal activity other than corporate worship, though none in which so many of the Christian community are so regularly involved. As part of our celebration of Easter, members of my local fellowship pile into cars, go to a particular few acres of woodland where the public has access only over Easter, and have a fun family walk through the woods: some 100 to 150 of our folk now make this trip, from babes in arms to grandmas – the young men and women climb a certain tree and practise enforced baptism in a certain ditch! It is a time of relaxation, of enjoying the trees and the primroses, of sheer fun, and I have no doubt whatever but that it is thoroughly therapeutic. Communal activity is good for your overall health!

C. The healing power of communal relations

'Therefore, as God's chosen people, holy and dearly loved, clothe yourselves with compassion, kindness, humility, gentleness and patience. Bear with each other and forgive whatever grievances you have against one another. Forgive as the Lord forgave you. And over all these virtues put on love, which binds them all together in perfect unity. Let the peace of Christ rule in your hearts, since as members of one body you were called to peace. And be thankful. Let the word of Christ dwell in you richly as you teach and admonish one another with all wisdom, and as you sing psalms, hymns and spiritual songs with gratitude in your hearts to God. And whatever you do, whether in word or deed, do it all in the name of the Lord Jesus, giving thanks to God the Father through him' (Colossians 3.12–17.

Perhaps more than any other, this passage has been used by God's Spirit to cause a revival of 'one anothering' in the local fellowship of believers and beyond. It amplifies the primary directive which is the Word of Jesus:

'A new command I give you: love one another. As I have loved you, so you must love one another. By this all men

will know that you are my disciples, if you love one another'
(John 13.34–35).

Paul insists that that command made new by the death of
Christ for us all is to be actualized in the personal relating of
members of the church one to another. Indeed, as the apostle
strives to find ways of showing young churches what the
practical outworkings of the Good News are, he produces a
whole series of 'one anothers', as for example:

'*Accept* one another just as Christ accepted you' (Romans
15.7);

'*Serve* one another in love' (Galatians 5.13);

Carry each other's burdens, and in this way you will fulfil the
law of Christ' (Galatians 6.2);

'*Be patient, bearing with* one another in love' (Ephesians 4.2);

'*Be kind and compassionate* to one another, *forgiving* one
another, just as in Christ God forgave you' (Ephesians
4.32);

'*Encourage* one another and *build* each other *up*' and 'always
try to *be kind* to each other' (I Thessalonians 5.11 and 15).

These are buttressed with exhortations in the negative form:

'Let us stop passing judgement on one another' (Romans
14.13);

'Let us not become conceited, provoking and envying each
other' (Galatians 5.26);

'Do not lie to each other' (Colossians 3.9).

This is a key strand of New Testament teaching, and has to
do directly with Christian fellowship, or what we are calling
the Kingdom priority of healing and pastoral care. We are
called to care for one another as Christ cared, and this calling
needs to be both taught and modelled by all those in leadership functions in the Church. The proliferation of house

groups or cells provides a good setting for such relating to be explored.

We can speak confidently of the healing power of Christians' relating because love, supremely, has healing properties. What so many who come looking for counselling truly need, the Christian community can and should be providing. The 'one anothers' or 'each others' can be grouped under 3 headings: love forgives, love shares, and love encourages.

Love forgives

What many people most need is to *experience* forgiveness: actually to forgive those who have wronged them, to forgive themselves for the wrong they hate themselves for, to be forgiven by others, and, as the heart of the gospel reveals, to know the forgiving love of God. It is not so much that forgiving needs to be *taught* as that it needs to be *experienced*: where should it be more in evidence than in the family of the Lord Who taught His followers to pray 'Father, forgive us . . . as we forgive others', Who prayed on the Cross for those who had crucified Him 'Father, forgive them', and Who alone makes our total forgiveness by God possible? A significant portion of the whole caring-counselling continuum is that of enabling resentful people to forgive and to be forgiven. To that end, it can be particularly helpful to *picture* forgiveness happening, and a powerful picture can be derived from the original biblical verbs for 'to forgive', being Hebrew *nasa* and *salach*, and Greek *aphiemi*. In each case, the root meaning has to do with moving something out of the way: you lift it out of the way, you send it away, you even hurl it away. Precisely that is the nub of forgiveness. What I need to do is to visualize what stands in the way between myself and my enemy, between myself and everybody else, between myself and me, or between myself and God. I need to acknowledge that it is an obstruction which, from my side, is made of and kept in place by my anger, resentment, hatred, despair, jealousy, pride, stubbornness, fear, cowardice, guilt, shame or whatever, being my reaction to what that 'other' did to me or is doing to me, or to what I *feel* went on or is going on. This is palpably sensitive territory because it has to do with those aspects of my being which I do not want to have to acknowledge; I would much prefer to dwell upon the sins of the 'other'. Unfortunately for me, however, to live behind such an obstruction is no joy at all: it casts its shadow over everything. What I need to decide is that I will put my energies to getting it shifted out of the way. More often than not, the obstruction has grown to such proportions and is made of such explosive materials that I need help: *the picture* is that of Jesus Christ and I together lifting that obstruction and throwing it right out of the way. Such an action costs me: I am full of thoughts to the effect that it was all the other person's fault anyway (and, indeed, in large part it may have been) but that alters nothing: my seething reactions build the barrier from my side, and my only way out of the oppression of it is to swallow my pride, pick up my courage, and ask the Lord to help me dismantle and entirely remove the barricade I built. Even during the writing of this section, a man came to me and said: 'I want to ask you to forgive me because I have been harbouring nasty thoughts towards you for over a year now; I want to tell you that they have now gone, and I ask you to forgive me.' We gave each other one of those very special hugs, I asked his forgiveness for any way in which I had contributed to his difficulty – and the angels rejoiced as another barrier was demolished. The way between us was clear again. Forgiveness is precisely that: the clearing of the way between ourselves and A. N. Other. Just as our Lord, at greatest cost, took the initiative to tackle the enormous obstruction of sin which blocked humankind off from God, so we, by His Spirit and with His love, are to take the initiative to tackle any blockage which prevents our free relating with others. In public worship and in housegroup prayertimes, there should regularly be space for the Lord to show us what stands between us and others, and to persuade us to do something about it, to forgive, to shift the blockage from our side with His help, and to take any appropriate steps of reconciliation. In our fellowshipping one with another, the moving of barriers should be a natural dimension of our being 'members one of another', and in our praying with one another, it is good to visualize mountains of grievance being dislodged and dumped in the sea as per Mark 11.23, a verse only two removed from this Word of Jesus:

'And when you stand praying, if you hold anything against

anyone, forgive him, so that your Father in heaven may forgive you your sins'.

Love shares

If forgiveness clears the way for real relating, sharing *enables* that real relating which effectively answers so many of our needs. Love yearns and learns to share itself, what it is, what it has. Just as 'accept one another', 'be patient, bearing with one another in love', and 'be compassionate to one another' are directly to do with a love which forgives, so 'serve one another in love', 'carry each other's burdens' and 'always try to be kind to one another' betoken a love which shares just because that is its nature. What, however, the Christian dynamic does is to take us beyond the level of practical kindnesses (which are lovely and always to be commended) into a more intimate sharing of ourselves. It is very difficult to put words on this, but one of the more fruitful ways, perhaps, is to employ the language of 'truth'. What the living Christ encourages are relationships which are 'truthful', that is, *full of truth*. It is instructive to note that the New Testament word for truth, *aletheia*, has as its root meaning the idea of *non-concealment*: the emphasis is not so much upon the listing of facts as upon the revealing of situations as they are, not so much upon being propositionally accurate as upon being openly honest. The model is Jesus Himself: according to John's testimony, Jesus is 'full of truth' (1.14) and, indeed, *is* the truth (14.6). Jesus declares that whoever *does* the truth 'comes into the light' (3.21), that 'true' worshippers worship the Father in spirit and in 'truth' (4.23), that those who really are His disciples will 'know the truth, and the truth will set (them) free' (8.32), and that after His departure, it is essential that they receive Him Who is 'the Spirit of Truth' for He guides 'into all truth' (16.13). The force of all this is that Jesus is the 'non-concealment' of God: He is the frank revelation of God, of Who and how God is, and, in the light of that 'truth', who and how man is. So often in the relating of human beings amongst themselves, there are 'hidden agendas': masks are worn, roles are played, white and not-so-white lies are told, at the expense of truth, of revealing things as they really are. In Christ there is no hidden agenda: all His 'truth' is out in the open with no distortion or deception. He is out in the open as who He is. One of the speech characteristics of Jesus faithfully relayed by all four Gospels is how He so often prefaces what He is about to reveal with the very emphatic '*Amen*' or even '*Amen, Amen*', the force of which is: 'I am sharing with you the truth, the whole truth, and nothing but the truth, and this is it'. So for example:

'For I tell you the truth, many prophets and righteous men longed to see what you see but did not see it, and to hear what you hear but did not hear it' (Matthew 13.17).

'I tell you the truth, this poor widow has put more into the treasury than all the others' (Mark 12.43).

'I tell you the truth, today you will be with me in paradise' (Luke 23.43).

'I tell you the truth, no-one can see the Kingdom of God unless he is born again' (John 3.3).

In each instance, there is frank disclosure, each opening up of a situation beginning with an emphatic 'amen'. That is how we are to be with God and with one another. We are to worship the Father in 'truth': that is to say, we open ourselves to Him, we share our 'truth' with Him, who we are, how we are, as we come before Him. We are to share with one another: we are to be found 'speaking the truth in love' (Ephesian 4.15), a much abused phrase which does *not* mean that I vent my wrath upon you by hitting you with 'truth' for your ill, but rather that I calmly open my heart and mind to yours, *for our good and especially yours!* In our small groups particularly, what should be happening under God is that we are enabled by His Spirit to share our 'truth' with one another: to be real, to be open, to be honest, and so, gradually and trustingly, to reveal to one another who and how we really are; only relationships based on non-concealment truth liberate, grow and bless. It is a sad fact that many wounds which fester to the point of needing counselling could have been healed within friendships founded upon truth.

Love encourages

Finally in relation to 'one anothering', we draw together 'teach and admonish one another with all wisdom' and 'encourage one another and build one another up' as being strands of the same love-dimension, namely that love encourages. If forgiveness clears the way to it and sharing in truth is the way into it, then encouragement is the intention of real relating. Love puts the accent on the other's wellbeing; love desires the other's good; love hopes to leave the other better than before. According to Mark chapter 6, the disciples were rowing across the Sea of Galilee and, due to a contrary wind, they were making heavy weather of it. Suddenly, Jesus is there: His voice rings out 'take courage! it is I! don't be afraid!' and somehow the wind drops and everything is better (Mark 6.50). That is a great illustration of how we are to be towards one another in Christ. We are to aim to put *heart* in one another, and particularly to seek to do so for those who are struggling. This principle applies to the strand of 'admonishing', too, a point which needs to be made because in some quarters admonition is being magnified out of all proportion to its actual place in the Christian scheme of things. Even when we think to admonish, it is the other's good and upbuilding that we must have in mind, so we must be very careful that we are not coming down on the other from some lofty position of our own uprightness: the intention of Christ, far from coming down on those who are in difficulty, is rather to lift them up, but always, as we have seen, through a basis of truth.

The relationship between counselling and the fellowship of the local church is particularly well expressed by Frank Lake in his magnum opus *Clinical Theology* (Darton, Longman and Todd, 1966):

'Our task is to reach the wounded self, or more often, wounded selves, whatever defensive system they are using for concealment.

We can say "You can come out now. Christ and we know you are there, and exactly how you feel. All your feelings are accepted, whether or not they were justified, as no doubt many of them were. So there is no need to hide any longer. If this is your dilemma, see how Christ has acted to deliver you from it. If that is your dilemma, his Cross has lighted a way through that one also. No amount of rage or pain of persecution or dread is beyond the power of the crucified Christ to heal''. Whatever went wrong with the primitive dynamic cycle of relationships in which the human spirit should have been founded, but where, in fact, it foundered and became a wreck, there is in Christ and His Church a new dynamic cycle of loving relatedness, a new creation of God, a new 'being', the man in Christ, and a new ''wellbeing'', the fullness of the Holy Spirit.

There would be no point in Christ's rescue work on the cross if He had not retained on earth a fellowship, His body, with its limbs or members, to offer a new dynamic cycle of relationships to those whose natural cycle had broken down, and who in any case, needed His divinity to replace their mortality. In this fellowship are shared the symbols of his continual self-giving. This too is the work which He achieved upon the cross. We are ''accepted through His blood'', we are ''brought near by the blood of His cross''.'

5

Our counselling toolkit

I belong to that section of humankind which, as they say, is not 'practical'. Even so, if you are a parent living in a family house with growing offspring and a limited budget, you need to be able to turn your hand to repair or strengthen quite a lot of things, and quickly! It is therefore essential that you have some tools. Unpractical by nature though I am, even I have a toolbox and in it, basic tools such as a hammer, a pair of pliers, a saw, and assorted screwdrivers and spanners; and somewhere along life's way, most probably as a youngster watching my father, I came to understand their uses and how to wield them. So it is in counselling: we should carry into the counselling sphere a box of tools which we have acquired and learned how to use. Unfortunately, however, even that apparently straightforward statement takes us directly into an area of conflict between Christian practitioners: namely, which 'tools' are legitimate for a *Christian* counsellor to use, and which are not? This is an issue to which trainee counsellors need to address themselves. The difficulty is this, that there is a massive library of books emanating from the world of psychotherapy presenting many different methods of counselling, many differing understandings of particular kinds of difficulties, and many different suggestions as to ways to effect alleviations or cures; furthermore, much of this literature is written by professionals who are not Christians, and who, in their written presentations, ignore or even look askance at Christian conviction: their presuppositions and premises are essentially humanist. Can it be legitimate for Christian counsellors to draw upon the experience and expertise of such practitioners? Just to complicate matters further, there is an increasing volume of *Christian* literture which assumes differing stances to this very problem: it will surprise nobody to learn that those who are theologically and biblically more liberal lean towards wholesale acceptance of what secular psychotherapy may have to offer, whereas the more conservative tend towards a wholehearted rejection of same. Most of us will plant our feet firmly somewhere between the two in order to attain not a weak compromise, but a position of strength from having given due weight to the claims and counter claims of each camp. In the next chapter, I shall be arguing that Christian counsellors should be looking unashamedly and expectantly to the scriptures and the living Word of God for breakthrough resources, a position which has been so positively strengthened by spiritual renewal and charismatic experience. Yet just as it would be foolish indeed to refuse to use a powerdrill on the grounds that Jesus did not use electricity in His carpentry, so it is foolish for us simply to spurn the data which modern psychotherapy has built up out of its vast experience of relating with troubled human beings and reflecting upon its own endeavours to help them. The expertise acquired offers the Christian counsellor certain tools – principles, methods, insights, connections, skills – which he must possess and which his Lord can show him how best to use. A very harsh thing needs to be interjected at this point: in these days, when people are encouraged to open their inner selves as the power of Christ is present to heal, irreparable harm can be done by the unequipped amateur, who, *very often to meet his own needs*, forces his way into somebody's private 'cellar' where explosive emotional materials have been buried in a live state: both parties can be blown apart. I acknowledge my own indebtedness to secular as well as Christian psychotherapy: I believe that, in practice, the modern ministry of Christian counselling is similarly indebted even if it is not always prepared to admit it. My base position is that there are some very important tools we may acquire and use in all the essential phases of the counselling process. For clarity's sake, I will first outline what the essential phases are, and then suggest some of the good tools which help the work of each phase.

The essential phases of the counselling process

Somebody has suggested that there must now be 200 different models for the counselling process, which is a ridiculously chaotic state of affairs. Mercifully for those of us involved in the kind of counselling normally required in the local Church context, a relatively straightforward *modus operandi* can be adopted and used as our guide. The intention of counselling, as we stated it from the outset in Chapter 1, is, through genuinely caring Christian relationship, to offer effective help to those who are experiencing real difficulties in some aspects of their emotions, thoughts and/or behaviour. We can move towards that objective through the three obvious phases of EXPLORING, CONNECTING and HEALING. Others may of course employ different words to denote the phases: that really does not matter as long as we are aware of the stages of the journey which must be made, and that we take each seriously rather than be anxious to rush on to the next phase or indeed to journey's end. It was Dr Frank Lake of 'Clinical Theology' fame addressing clergymen, who said that it takes a deal of time for the deep things to be drawn up from the well of the soul, and that too many clergy buckets come up from a shallow place and much too quickly at that! Our counselling objective, if it is to be achieved, will be achieved *through* a real relationship between counsellor and counselee. Although that may seem obvious, it is itself an important finding of modern psychotherapy which I drew your attention to in Chapter 3 when I made reference to the pioneering research of Carl Rogers, subsequently built upon by Truaux and Carkhuff. Prior to their work bursting upon the scene in the 1960s, the assumption had tended to be that the counsellor was the expert who knew and the counselee was the layman who did not: what was required was for the former to enlighten the latter. I suspect that, even so, many real and warm relationships did in fact occur between counsellor and counselee, but the relevance of that was not perceived until Rogers and co., investigating professional psychotherapy's apparently high failure rate, discovered that the more genuine the relationship between counsellor and counselee, the more seemed to be accomplished. That finding stands firm today: effective counselling presupposes a warmly human relationship between counsellor and counselee, though one which is targeted towards the end in view, namely the healing and the personal growth of the latter. The phases of counselling are *both* for the building of an effectively therapeutic relationship *and* for the accomplishing of the healing and the growth. I will now outline the specific shape and intention of each phase so that we may then identify some of the tools appropriate for the work to be undertaken in each.

Exploring

The task in this initial stage is twofold: it is, on the one hand, that of beginning to establish why the counselee requires counselling, and on the other hand, of beginning to establish real rapport. Taking the first part of that equation first, the counselee will be aware of his own reason for seeking counselling: there is likely to be a presenting problem – that is to say, some clear difficulty in the present living of life – and the counsellor will gently begin to elicit what that difficulty might be. The counsellor will also seek to enable the counselee to release any bottled up feelings he may have in connection with what has happened or is happening, because what really disturbs us is not so much an event or a situation of itself, but our emotional reaction to it. Furthermore, the way we react to particular situations may very well have roots in our past history, and gently patient exploring of that also will usually be called for. At the same time, the counselee is not going to divulge his personal secrets if he does not respect and trust the counsellor, so clearly the whole manner and method of the counsellor does need to be such as to inculcate confidence, openness and encouragement in the counselee, in order that any painful areas which need exploring may be brought out of hiding. In this connection, I developed a teaching paper for all members of my local fellowship, a section of which was headed: 'I shan't open up to you if' and there then followed nine 'ifs,' thus:

1) IF, even as I begin to talk, I see that you are fidgeting and unrelaxed: your mind is somewhere else, you are thinking of where you are going next, of what you still have to do after

me – you haven't got time or concentration for what I need from you. . . .

2) IF, even as I began to talk, a warning light flashes and I realize that my feel about you is that you will probably tell somebody else anything I tell you. . . .

3) IF, even as I begin to talk, I sense that you are unhealthily nosey: you are asking me questions not to help me but to satisfy your own curiosity. . . .

4) IF, as I begin to put words on my need, I find that you just cannot shut up and listen to me: every time I lapse into silence, to recollect, to feel, to ponder my next step, you butt in; you can't cope with silence, you don't know how to listen. . . .

5) IF, as I begin to put words on my need, you switch the conversation to yourself: 'Oh yes, I do know what you mean: I get anxious about such and such myself, why I remember when I – I – I – I.' Me, I shall fall silent and let you get on with yourself. . . .

6) IF, as I begin to put words on my need, you interrupt smartly with some quick, easy solution: 'just pray about it, Peter; it will be alright.' You insult me by giving me a plaster when I need surgery. . . .

7) IF, as I do open up, I sense that you are being shocked by what I am telling you: you are judging me, you are sitting there thinking: 'how disgraceful that a Christian, yes and a Minister too, should feel like that. . . .'

8) IF, as I do open up, I discover that you cannot cope with the real me I am letting you see: you are getting frightened, you are getting embarrassed, you are getting hostile. . . .

9) IF, as I do open up, I realise that you cannot cope with my particular real need: the truth is that my particular anxiety is making *you* feel anxious; you cannot help me, you cannot cope with my darkness because you haven't even come to terms with your own. . . .

Connecting

Whilst the word includes the essential connecting of counsellor and counselee in mutual respect and genuine transaction, the main weight of it here is in making a connection between the counselee's present difficulty with the emotions, thoughts and actions it currently arouses, and his own personal history. Such 'connection' can be diagrammatically depicted as a 'T', the horizontal representing the counselee's present life setting, the vertical representing his personal history, and the join being not only the present difficulty but also the 'connection' to be perceived by the counsellor. Past deficiencies, failures or interruptions of love in the family unit during the years of the counselee's infancy or childhood; particular relationship events perceived to be dreadful (and they may have been) in the forms of betrayal, conflict, defeat, failure, or humiliation; catastrophic events occurring without any warning, in the form of bereavement, parental separation or severe illness; a network of relationships and/or circumstances which inhibited the child or did him down or frightened him or ruined his prospects – there are the proverbial 1001 possibilities. The turning point for the counselee however, may well be the making of a connection never made before.

Healing

If exploring has led to connecting, then connecting leads on towards healing: appropriate rehabilitation needs to be agreed and put into motion, and here again there are many possibilities. One school of theory will insist that what needs to be done is to change the *feelings*, another, the *thoughts*, and a third, the *behaviour* of the one who is receiving counselling. What that scenario really says is twofold: first, that sometimes the way out of difficulty is primarily a change in feelings OR in thoughts OR in behaviour, and, second, that the human being is a complex entity, and you cannot wholly separate out feelings from thoughts from actions. A significant positive move in the one will trigger good things in the others also. In his manual for Christian 'people-helpers', *A Friend in Need*, Selwyn Hughes introduces his readers to 'irrational ideas' which need to be replaced by rational ones. His first example is: 'I must be loved and accepted by those who are most important to me, and (I must) live up to their expectations.' Very often the connecting material here is that of parents who *seemed* (in fact, they may or may not have) to make their love for their child conditional: 'We will love you *if* you reach the mark we set you' is the message received, so whenever the child fails or is rebuked or otherwise chastized, he feels deeply anxious as to whether he is really loved at all; as a result, he may well redouble his efforts to 'earn' the love he needs. What that childhood dynamic too often leaves is a legacy for the adult of feelings, thoughts and behaviour all tyrannized by 'must', which makes that adult's significant relationships a minefield for him rather than an oasis, so that his inner being is frequently stressed: any hiccup in an important relationship assumes the nature of a major disaster. Now it is clearly arguable that healing could occur by working to replace the irrational idea with a rational one, but it is also arguable that the way through could be to acknowledge the intense emotional underlay and work to change that, or to plan for change in actual relating with a significant friend. There cannot be a law, and we must not be slaves to any theory; we will need to go on developing and praying for a sensitivity and wisdom which shows us where the break-through can be made. So then, in this healing phase, there may be emotional bondages to be broken, tyrannical mind tapes to be erased and replaced with gentle truthful ones, particular manageable behaviour changes to be taken, reconciliation moves to be made, in order that steps are cut which enable the counselee to take the Lord's hand, to climb out of the miry pit, to stand on firm rock, and to sing the new song which the Lord has given.

So what tools have the professionals fashioned and improved which lay counsellors may take and learn to use? I shall forthwith patent my own silly names for them.

Tools for exploring

A. The HEARometer
This delicate device measures how deeply you listen and how accurately you hear as opposed to how much you talk! In the world of espionage, political or industrial, it is remarkable to note the application and ingenuity with which one side will develop and set in place ever more sophisticated instrumentation in order to listen in to the other side. Fortunately, something of the same endeavour is also put into the development of hearing aids so that the deaf or partially deaf may listen in a little to the world around them. What counsellors need to be convinced of, and over and over again, is that their key tool from the start of the counselling journey is going to be their own skill at listening. All the counselling manuals emphasize that but unfortunately too many would-be counsellors switch off from it very quickly: 'of course we must listen – but then we spend much of our lives listening already, don't we'? The answer is really 'no'. We spend much of our time *half* listening and *part* hearing, but only a small percentage of people are good listeners. Even in a one-to-one situation, most of us are busy organizing our minds to frame our reply before the speaker is a quarter of the way through what he wants to say just to start things off! Very few of us can stay quiet during a silence which the other needs in order to put words on deeper feelings and thoughts. Most of us are quick to move in upon the other's experience with copious material from our own experience. Often to assuage their own growing anxiety as someone begins to outline a problem to them, Christians move in too quickly with a neat solution – a scripture verse, a little prayer – and make their exit. After years and years of counselling experience, I still spend too many moments in counselling situations telling myself to shut up and listen. We are describing here real listening, which comes from giving yourself to the wellbeing of the counselee, from being committed to wanting and seeking his good. This book is not itself a teach-yourself-counselling kind of manual, so I must limit myself to the major point that we need to put ourselves on the Hearometer and monitor our own listening capacity: I can tell you that the experience is akin to getting

on your scales – what it says is not what you would like it to say!

Listening can be *learned*. It is to some extent an art which can be scientifically analysed and therefore taught. For example, *reflective listening* is a great aid to effective counselling. What it means is that as the counselee begins to venture to put some words on some dominant feelings, you aid that process by reflecting back, in your own words, what you have heard: in that way, of course, the counselee can correct you if you are not hearing him, and that is important, but the real fruit of reflective listening is that as you summarize the feelings accurately, the counselee knows that you understand something of his inner world of feelings and meanings, and he is therefore encouraged to continue and to reveal more of what needs to be brought to the surface. I would encourage counsellors and would-be counsellors in the churches to read and re-read material on listening skills, and also to look for a counselling course where, in a small group, they can partici- pate in role play and observe it, and thus sharpen the skills of unhurried, unanxious, committed and empathic listening.

B. The FEELometer

This highly sophisticated instrument measures how well you get in touch with another's real feelings, and, as importantly, how well you are already in touch with your own. We Chri- stians have a lengthy manual on how to fail the FEELometer test: it is called the Book of Job! In fact, chapters 4 to 25 depict counsellors Eliphaz, Bildad and Zophar comprehens- ively failing the HEARometer test: they began well by sitting with Job in silence (chapter 2.13), but as soon as Job begins to express intense thoughts and emotions, crying out for some understanding and support, the three 'friends' prove incap- able of hearing him, for they are imprisoned in a theological straitjacket which does not permit that questioning of the justice of things which Job *has* to express. That already is a sober warning to Christians, particularly if they fiercely adhere to that 'school' of theology: will you listen to someone who needs to shout at the very truth you most highly prize? However, the Job manual goes from bad to so much worse. Elihu has been listening in: he has had time to observe and reflect, but the writer of the book is so astute at this point: his introduction to Elihu is this:

> 'But Elihu became very angry with Job for justifying himself rather than God. He was also angry with the three friends, because they had found no way to refute Job, and yet had condemned him. Now Elihu had waited before speaking to Job because they were older than he. But when he saw that the three men had nothing more to say, his anger was aroused. So Elihu said . . .' (Job 32.2–6).

What that describes is Elihu totally failing the FEELometer test. His agenda is not Job's very real difficulty and need, his agenda is *his own anger*, and Job is left aching and frustrated in his anguish. No wonder he cries out (and I employ here a marvellous piece of translation I chanced upon somewhere):

> 'Miserable plasterers are you all!' (Job 16.2).

Frankly, there are too many Christian plasterers about – too entrenched, too angry, too insecure, too repressed themselves to be able to cope with the deepest feelings of another; they generally seek to cover their own anxieties by offering a too quick, too neat, too simple solution which serves only to plaster over what is actually serious structural damage. We need to learn to get in touch with our own feelings: we too have a personal history which leaves us with areas of vulnerability which, when put under pressure, can generate anger, fear, lust, despair or guilt in us ourselves, and we had better be a familiar and accepting acquaintance of our own emotional make-up before we actually put ourselves under pressure by encouraging a counselee to share his. Otherwise, our name will be Elihu.

All that said, it is imperative that we develop skills in enabling others to reveal and ventilate their innermost emotions, for it is desperately difficult for many people to be able to do unaided what needs to be done. We must learn to listen to *feelings*. Often camouflaged in the volume of words the counselee speaks is an emotional message: 'I am terribly frightened', 'I am hurting so badly', 'I am hopelessly confused', 'I am utterly alone', 'I am fearfully angry'. If we can decipher the code, we can enable these destructive emotions or 'truths' to come to the light and have their poison drawn off. Another kind of language we need to learn to interpret is that of the counselee's body language – hand movements, facial expressions, change of voice, shifts in posture, eye contact, and so on. We speak that language ourselves, of course, and should be able to communicate acceptance, understanding, warmth, relaxation and encouragement. Yet another language is to pick up what message the counselee is sending through our own reactions to him. There are counselling sessions where we appear to be getting nowhere by way of inviting responses and disclosures from the counselee himself. Then can be the time to ask the question: 'what is my own emotional reaction to this person?' Eugene Kennedy, in his most helpful guide *On Becoming a Counsellor* says that the most common 'messages' counselees put into their counsellors are: 'I feel helpless', 'I feel angry', 'I feel frightened' and 'I feel depressed'. Having of course checked that those are not our own problems, it may very well be that we are experiencing how the counselee feels even though he is not prepared or able to say it in words; in some instances, mind you, it is all part of the 'game' the counselee is playing: the depressive, for example, may be wanting to *prove* that you cannot help him any more than anyone or anything else can, because his 'truth' is that everything is hopeless, so nothing can be done. Nonetheless, if we read accurately the language within our own reactions, we are being handed a passkey into the emotional state of the coun- selee: as in all other contexts, so here, too, passkeys should be used very responsibly and only with permission sought and given. Furthermore, we need to develop our skill at enabling wounded people to give full vent to hitherto suppressed feelings, even if their airing of them is with much passion or agitation. I have always admired the foresight of the Japanese factory which gave over one room to punchbag likenesses of the managers; any employee was free to go into that room and get rid of his feelings about any particular manager by beating the living daylights out of his likeness! There is an important principle there of getting powerful negative feelings out into the open and expressed: perhaps each church building should have such a room with punchbag effigies of the pastor, elders and cell leaders! Christian counsellors will also need to understand that some who seek their aid will have explosive feelings towards God, and they should not be shocked when these too are vented: Scripture gives us good precedents – in, for example, Job's ventilations towards God as his 'counsellors' listen:

'I will complain in the bitterness of my soul.
Will you never look away from me
   or let me alone for an instant?
Why have you made me your target? (7.11,19–20)
Does it please you to oppress me,
   to spurn the work of your hands
   while you smile on the schemes of the wicked? (10.3).
What do I gain by not sinning?' (35.3)

It is not within the scope of this book to teach such skills but rather to make the plea that our local church counsellors and carers are persuaded to recognize that there are skills which can be practised, sharpened and honed, particularly in a training group or supervision context.

Tools for connecting and healing

If, for a moment, we allow those words to stand for diagnosis and treatment in respect of physical diseases, we will gladly acknowledge and avail ourselves of the tremendous range of highly sophisticated instruments which have been developed for those purposes. What we need to see is that parallel equipment is available for diagnosis and therapy in respect of emotional and mental uneases, and many diagnostic and therapeutic skills or, as I am depicting them, 'tools' are available to us to increase the efficacy of our counselling. As in the physical realm, so now in the emotional – mental, the degree of specialization increases. Rather than generalize, I choose to illustrate my contention by describing just two tools which have been handed to me from the world of professional psychotherapy and for which I already have cause to be grateful. The first is particularly helpful in 'connecting' and the second in 'healing', each in relation to a specific scenario.

A. *An approach to homosexuality*

The first scenario is that of homosexuality. Battle is now well and truly joined in our society as to whether certain people are homosexual by their very nature and should thus be encouraged to be who they are and to be free to form at least lifelong partnerships with one of their own kind, or whether there is no such person as a homosexual born and bred, and therefore homosexual orientation, let alone practice, is to be viewed as aberrant and always requiring therapy. It is not within my province here to examine all the evidence marshalled to support the one view or the other. My purpose is to acknowledge gratefully that the published reflections of Dr Elizabeth Moberly, a professional specialist in psychoanalytic developmental psychology, have greatly helped me in counselling those who are unsure of their sexual identity or are already overtly homosexual but sufficiently ill at ease about that to seek counsel. I first came across her work through an article in the *Expository Times* of June 1985 given to me by a 'homosexual' much helped by it. The article prompted the acquiring of her book: *Homosexuality: a New Christian Ethic*, published by James Clarke & Co. of Cambridge in 1983. In lay language, Dr Moberly's contention is that the psychological data in relation to homosexual orientation and practice contains one common strand: namely, that there was a same-sex love-deficiency in earlier years. A homosexual man is one who is looking to fulfil his need for loving relationship with a man because that did not happen with his own father. A homosexual woman is similarly looking to resolve needs which arise from a deficiency in the development of her love relationship with her mother. This does not necessarily impute blame to the parent – a temporary severance through serious illness, for example, could cause such developmental failure. The importance of this finding is that the homosexual's need for same-sex friendship is *legitimate*, though to seek to form and express same-sex friendship through sexual activity is as utterly inappropriate as sexual activity would have been between the father and his son or the mother and her daughter.

The same-sex need being legitimate, it is completely unsatisfactory merely to counsel celibacy or marriage, the traditional Christian 'cures' for homosexuality, since neither addresses the real and legitimate need which is for same-sex acceptance and friendship. Dr Moberly's contention is that what is required is precisely such an accepting friendship with a person of the same sex, but a friendship that understands that sexual activity is wholly inappropriate and, indeed, from a Christian standpoint based upon the Scriptures, totally wrong. What this can mean is that the counsellor be that friend. What needs to be explored will be both the original same-sex deficit and the consequent ambivalence the counselee will have in all same-sex relationships. The counselee needs to understand that he or she is struggling with a legitimate developmental need rather than some terrible sexual deviancy, and the way through to positive heterosexuality or positive celibacy can only be by way of that need being first met.

My own testimony is that counselling along those lines of connecting present difficulty with past same-sex love deficiency has been both illuminating and fruitful. It is an example of how stimulating an aid a new piece of research can be for a lay Christian counsellor, and how effective a tool it can become.

B. *An approach to depression*

Depression is the everyman illness, a bout of which few of us will entirely escape in our lifespan. It is no easy task to counsel someone who is in the grip of a neurotic depression: he may find it very difficult to do much work with you and you may have to be much more active than usual, despite the fact that something of his bleak world may well settle within you. You will almost certainly have it in the back of your mind that there may well be anger lurking in the background, almost certainly connected with some form of loss, although you will also know that it would be counterproductive to look for that anger too soon. All this said, understood and gradually revealed, what is your stance vis-à-vis such a depression? What profile of healing do you see for what can continue to be a wasteland of despair? In this respect I am particularly indebted to the work of Dr Dorothy Rowe as presented in her book *Depression* published by Routledge in 1983. Her conclusion from a wealth of professional experience and data is the premiss of her book, being.

'Depression is a prison which we build for ourselves. Just as we build it, so we can unlock the door and let ourselves out'.

Dr Rowe then proceeds to elaborate upon that in three illuminating sections, thus:

How I build the Prison

'It is not things in themselves which trouble us, but the opinions we have about those things.' (Epictatus)

I build the prison by holding fast to the following opinions which I call 'truth':

1. No matter how good and nice I appear to be, I am really bad, evil, valueless, unacceptable to myself and to other people.

2. Other people are such that I must fear/hate/envy them.

3. Life is terrible and death is worse.

4. Only bad things happened to me in the past and only bad things will happen to me in the future.

5. It is wrong to get angry.

6. I must never forgive anyone, least of all myself.

Why I won't leave the prison.

1. I have high standards.

2. I am a sensitive person.

3. I will not risk being rejected.

4. I prefer to expect the worst rather than risk disappointment.

5. My problems are greater than anyone else's,

OR

anyone who hasn't got my problem has no problem at all.

6. I would think there was something wrong if I weren't suffering.

7. Besides, it's safe inside the prison.

8. And I am right, even if I am suffering for it.

Suppose I did want to leave the prison. . . .

1. Do not play the 'yes, but . . .' game.

2. Treat yourself kindly.

3. Put pills in your power.

4. Create a peaceful place within yourself.

5. Risk putting some trust in yourself and others.

6. Find someone to talk things over with.

7. Discover that there is nothing wrong with seeing the funny side of things.

8. Dare to explore new ways of thinking and doing.

That constitutes a very firm but positive stance which, when the time comes, gives the depressed person hope: there is room for change and scope for work. Christians can be over-sympathetic: depressives actually need not so much sympathy as hope, and Dr Rowe's guidance has stood me in good stead.

I hope that this chapter will have substantiated my stance that we Christian lay counsellors and carers have much to garner from our professional counterparts, secular or Christian: there are some very fine 'tools' available for our use. However, a final comment needs to be one of warning: beware of technique taking over from warm and real relating; beware of treating the counselee as your guinea pig in an experiment to test your latest acquired piece of research; and beware of trying to manipulate a counselling transaction so that it conforms to your own theory. This is why I have called these aids 'tools': tools are neutral; what they do depends upon the hands that use them. A hammer is a hammer, no more and no less; it can cause a great deal of damage in the wrong hands but be very constructive when used wisely and appropriately. I hope I don't sound 'pi' when I say that the best thing to do with counselling tools is to enlist the advice of Him Who is master carpenter and wonderful counsellor.

6

Our spiritual renewal

_____

I recall vividly from student days a huge argument between a fellow student and myself about lovemaking, both of us arguing out of the sweet innocence of being very long on theory but entirely without actual experience! He, being a student of the Sciences, argued painstakingly for technique, and I, as the representative of the Arts, spoke passionately for intuition and spontaneity. Today, I hope I would be a better listener prepared to accept the good in his arguments. That said and done (and following a love affair of more than 25 years of marriage), I would still put up a spirited defence of my original position: there is now even more 'technique' about, but what it so often issues in is *sex*-making, not *love*-making. I hold that love has depths unreached by analysis or technique: there is another language, a deeper communication which has to do with intuition, atmosphere, instinct, soul. In the chapter preceding this one, I gave good ground to the technique argument, not to be suitably charitable, but out of conviction which I trust is well founded upon wisdom; in this chapter, however, the 'Arts', as it were, now stand their own ground fearless of any invasion plans the Sciences may conceive.

In Section A of this Book, I presented the outlines of a biblical and theological foundation for the counselling ministry in the local church. So far in this Section B, I have indicated two primary resources for that ministry: the local church as a therapeutic community, and the expertise of professional practitioners as our guide. This, however, is a book in a series concerning *Renewal Issues in the Church* and it is now time for me to formulate my conviction that renewal by the Holy Spirit contributes a unique and vital dimension to Christian counselling. Why should that be? What is spiritual renewal? It has to be said that in all generations there are those Christians who deeply abide in the Lord and are thereby renewed day by day, but there are generations wherein the majority have lost the immediacy of relationship with God: there is then a distance and a powerlessness about their discipleship. It has been so in British Christianity for too long now. Currently, however, there is the possibility of a widespread liberation, although a simple statement like that is sufficient to provoke entrenched resistance or even open opposition: I know a little about the process, for I was for some years forcibly on the side of the opposition. What is crucial is to work through to what the essence of spiritual renewal is and is not: it is *not* in essence changing worship styles, it is *not* a free-for-all, it is *not* spiritual superiority, although it may *look* like all of those, especially to less than sympathetic eyes. So what is it? There are many different kinds of language one may use to give others a sight of the quintessential of renewal: I shall use this one, that the Lord is freshly inviting us to give to his Spirit freedom to work through both the left and the right sides of our brain, a freedom largely denied to Him for decades, so that the living Word of God might again be seen, heard and experienced by His People and in the nation.

I understand that, in layman's language, the left side of the brain is the domain of the rational, and the right side that of the intuitive, these corresponding to the masculine and the femine dimensions respectively; for completeness, each person needs both in good and co-operative working order. On that reckoning, the church in this country has been overdominated by the left side of the brain: the world of theology and of church life has been ordered along the lines of our own reasoning powers; the local church's programme, for example, has been formulated on the basis of good ideas thought to be generally in accord with what God would wish. I do not despise that: I ministered on that kind of basis for several years, and I refuse to allow anyone to invalidate those years, because at their centre was a stubborn commitment to Christ as the Way, the Truth and Life, and I did not then know (although sometimes I wondered) that there was much better wine available. When the challenge of charismatic renewal and restoration had for a good long time been beating at my door, *and* I had fully exercised my mind in stand-up fights with charismatics and, importantly, by facing every significant Biblical passage concerning the Holy Spirit (under the disciplined critical guidance of Dr James Dunn in his magnificent *Jesus and the Spirit*), *and* had alternately fought and pleaded with God, I finally reached a place where I knew I had to lay down my mind on the altar of God, and particularly lay down my unanswered questions. My ideas and my questions had been limiting God's activity within me and my ministry. I had to learn that it was *His* ministry: He was gracious as ever, and when it was time (months after I had felt it was high time!) He filled me with His Spirit as I had never known except at the time of my conversion. At the time of my conversion, I did not know what was happening to me and, because nobody in the church told me, I did not go on being filled with the Spirit. Now, however, I *loved* the Lord with my mind, and offered my reasoning powers to be a *servant* of His living Word. That, however, is only one side of the story, the left-hand side! I had always had a predilection for the Arts with a love for language, poetry and imagery, yet one's theological training had seemed to be so scientific and unimaginative. Now the Lord began to release my intuitive capacity, that is to say, the feminine aspect of personality (which men are so often taught *not* to reveal). I began to experience the intimacy of 'Abba', and to receive living Word from God, often rich in imagery. The Scripture with its treasure store of imagery sprang to life: I had never really been grasped by how *visual* God's Word is when He communicates with us by His Spirit: in just the opening chapter of Isaiah, for example, the Lord pictures Judah as a rebellious child (verse 2), a badly wounded person (verse 5) and a harlot (verse 21). Those themes are aided and abetted by similes:

'The daughter of Zion is left like a shelter in a vineyard, like a hut in a field of melons, like a city under siege' (1:8)

and by metaphors:

'I will thoroughly *purge away your dross* and remove all your impurities' (1:25).

Indeed, God's supreme living Word is Jesus, *the* visual aid in all history. Furthermore, the gifts of the Spirit such as the selection given by Paul in I Corinthians 12:7–11 flow through liberated intuition, which is why, I suspect, that when a fellowship begins to enter the renewal experience, the first people to be baptized (afresh) in the Spirit and to move in the gifts of the Spirit are likely to be receptive women. The gifts of the Word of Knowledge, the Word of Wisdom and the Discernment of Spirits, for example, flow directly through intuition open to and filled by the Spirit: try as you may, and as those who are prisoners of the rational must, you cannot analyse those: they are *given*; they *happen*; you *know*. It is all of a piece with the classic scenario wherein a husband finds the house which has everything which his wife stipulated: he takes her to see it, she steps in the front door (if she gets that far!) and she says: 'No, this is not the house for us'. The husband is nonplussed and not best pleased: 'why not?' he demands to know, 'you haven't even looked over it yet, and it's exactly what you said you wanted'. She cannot satisfy him, for she cannot explain: it is not a rational or logical decision, it is intuitive: she *knows*, and that is that. So it is with the aforementioned gifts, and with the others too, those of extra faith, dynamic powers, healing, prophecy and tongues: they are spiritual *events*; they obey no laws of logic and are incapable of rational explanation; they are not irrational, they are *supra* rational. We are more than ready to read the sonorous words from Isaiah 55:

> 'For my thoughts are not your thoughts, neither are your ways my ways', declares the Lord. 'As the heavens are higher than the earth, so are my ways higher than your ways and my thoughts than your thoughts',

but we are not really into *believing* them: we do not permit the Lord to have thoughts and ways which actually exceed our own. That passage continues with the divine assertion that the Word of the Lord will not return to Him empty. The specific Word in question was: 'You will go out' (of Babylonian captivity) and, remarkably, some of the people did: many more, however, missed the thought and the way of the Lord, staying put in Babylon on the grounds that, in the circumstances, that was the patently sensible thing to do. They missed God's future for His chosen People. 'Charismata' are the Lord's thoughts and ways revealed to us, given for our good and to accomplish His purpose. I propose to give one astonishing example out of the recent past, but first, let me point out that the adjective I naturally reached for was 'astonishing': when we describe what God thinks and does as 'astonishing', what we are revealing is how little used we are to expecting or allowing the Lord to move amongst us beyond the thoughts and ways of our own rationalism; it has been so from the beginning – witness how the people encountering the ministry of Jesus spent so much of their time being astonished! (look up Mark 1.22, 27; 2.12; 5.20, 42; 6.2, etc. etc.). None of this is astonishing to God: to Him, it is perfectly natural. Let me now give you my 'astonishing' example. During a Sunday service, a church member came to the platform and said to me: 'This sounds silly, but all I have in my mind tonight are the two words "shoplifting" and "Woolworths" '. So we spoke the words to the assembled company. In the congregation was a person who, it transpired, was passing through Bedford, had stopped off to see a friend, had chanced to come to our Service, and had stolen some articles from Woolworths the week before. That Word of Knowledge was God's thought, God's way, designed to stop that person in his/her tracks: I can assure you that it did just that! That event was *super*natural, *supra* rational, but we are so permeated by the scientism of our age that we do not like to acknowledge that; we cannot believe that there is anything which the left side of our brain cannot entirely explain, so we kill the supernatural by way of a thousand qualifications. Already, in renewal circles, I see eyes that were cleared by the Spirit of God growing cataracts of rationalism all over again. In making such comments, I know that I am living dangerously: let me insist again that I am not anti-reason or anti-intellect, rather I am anti the arrogance and, indeed, the blasphemy, which says that my mind is the arbiter of what God can or cannot do, that the human mind has the measure of the infinite God. In my first chapter, I listed what

I see to be the Kingdom priorities of Jesus. I believe that spiritual renewal is directly relevant to all of those, because each needs to be directed and empowered by living Word from God through the Spirit, as in the ministry of Jesus. The Lord God has mighty thoughts and mighty ways, quite beyond ours, when it comes to Prayer and Worship, Evangelism and Community Involvement, Teaching and Discipling, and particularly, given the province of this study, when it comes to Healing and Pastoral Care. In chapter 3, I made it very clear that our reliance as counsellors should be upon the Lord as we seek to counsel, and I now need to establish why. First, however, I shall set out my stall by telling some truth.

Telling the truth about our failure

Although the church I tend in Bedford is relatively large and strong in resources for a local Baptist Church (it has a committed membership of 300), the truth is that in our counselling ministry, our 'failures' outnumber our 'successes'. Within the membership, within the wider orbit of the church's network of contacts, and within the number of those 'passing through' at any given point in time, there are by no means only a few who have very real problems when it comes to coping with life: we are able to bring temporary relief to the majority but honesty compels me to report that, in far too many instances, the underlying mental, emotional or spiritual problem remains undealt with; a few months pass, another unwelcome turn of events occurs, and the persons concerned are struggling once more as the 'buried alive' difficulty is triggered yet again. I am referring here to those whom we seek to counsel for as long as seems right or fruitful and with whom and for whom we pray, and yet only first-aid, rather than the necessary surgery, appears to be accomplished. In addition, there are those who evidently have serious difficulties with living, with relationships, with themselves and/or with God, and whose condition we do not really touch at all: I have had to learn to face my own guilt-feelings about that, as we simply do not have the resources of personnel and time to take them on in the committed way they need. Sometimes our available resources are so stretched that we have to decide, in cold blood as it were, that in regard to this and that evidently deeply disturbed person, we will as far as possible let sleeping dogs lie, hoping that those persons will not actually demand help. The queue of those who need care and counsel never seems to diminish: recently I had reason to look at a random list of some 90 of our congregation, members and adherents, and my own pastoral knowledge told me that 19 have quite serious difficulties with living (6 of those have already had professional psychiatric help) and that a further 11 live in highly stressful circumstances which adversely affect them. That means that 1 in 3 have considerable problems, and since I do not know everybody that well, the reality is probably somewhat worse. It is no wonder then, though it is no credit to me, that occasionally I see a newcomer in our midst, I take a good hard look, and my heart sinks because I know I am looking at yet another 'problem' – yes, a precious child of God for whom Christ died, but pastorally yet another 'problem'. During the 24 hours before I fled from Bedford with no forwarding address to write this chapter, I was found by: a 'wanderer', being a seriously disturbed drug addict who had discharged himself from the mental hospital into which the police had taken the time and trouble to get him; a mother who showed some of the signs of hysterical personality; a fellow pastor whose marriage and ministry were threatening to cave in under the pressures put on him by others; and a young person whose head was full of thoughts and fears about homosexuality. What can I do but give too little attention to each? There are those who depart disappointed or even disgusted; mercifully, there are more who are blessed by the counsellor's concern or commitment even if their underlying problems are unresolved. John Wimber's ministry to needy people has been very powerful; I have been there myself as a witness; yet what most remains with me is this big man's honest admission: 'many are blessed; few are changed'. Thus far, that is my testimony also. I feel constrained to add that my admittedly limited experience of people who have sought professional psychiatric or psychotherapeutic aid suggests similar findings, although these practitioners are often dealing with patients who are so severely disturbed as to be in a psychotic condition. All of that said, and Christian integrity demands that it be said, I can now lay down alongside it something very different.

The impact of spiritual renewal upon Christian counselling

Mark chapter 2 and verses 1–12 is really a perfect miniature of the whole mission ministry of Jesus. The healing of the man in body, mind and spirit is a sign of God's Kingdom breaking in through Jesus; that is an unwelcome shock for those who have encapsulated the living God within their own theological straitjacket (a warning yet again to us Christians), and it is a mind-blowing occurrence for the ordinary folk who are, as I observed earlier, 'amazed'. Something of unusual proportion is taking place. What is it? God's Word uttered in Christ is changing a man's whole situation. This happens through a combination of *extraordinary perception* and *extraordinary power*: Jesus sees that the man's real need is not merely the *presenting* problem of his paralysis but the *hidden* problem of his unforgivenness; the problem has to do with thoughts and emotions, doubtless fuelled by popular notions that continuing paralysis bespoke great sinfulness. Jesus not only perceives, He has the power to forgive, demonstrably so, because the paralysis disappears. The Father gives His Son extraordinary perception and power by the Spirit to heal and to open the doors of the Kingdom to those who witness the Word in action. We can say that there is a faith-factor ('When Jesus saw their faith' 2.5), though it is certainly not quantifiable. What spiritual renewal effects is that we are taken into that place which is in any case our Christian birthright where Christ is present as Lord in the Spirit. He is present with all His perception and power in his Body, the church, longing to bless people with the blessings of the Kingdom. There is a faith factor: He does seek the trust of the people, encouraging us to be like the child who goes to his Father expecting good things, for if we earthly parents, with our many imperfections, yet know how to give good things to our children, *how much more* will our heavenly Father give good things to His children who come to Him naturally, confidently, expectantly (Matthew 7.11). Given such an environment of expectancy, He acts. Father-God acts through His Son by the Spirit. In relation to counselling ministry, if we look to Him trustingly, He will input directly with perception and power, not to enhance our counselling reputation, but for the good of His inhibited or damaged children. It is this dimension of direct supernatural supra-rational input which has been missing: we have not had the child's relationship with Father; we have known about it, but we have not allowed the Spirit of God through the work of Christ to take us into it. When we do, the Kingdom breaks in. What I must now do is to illustrate what can happen in relation to caring-counselling: as I do, please remember what I wrote earlier in this chapter about many 'failures'.

A. *From the Father, through the Son, by the Spirit – into our exploring*

Jenny suffers from that mysterious disease known as multiple sclerosis, 'mysterious' because its symptoms come and go, ebb and flow. Sometimes Jenny needed two sticks in order to walk, sometimes none, and, given such an erratic pattern of symptoms, other people could be less than sympathetic. During the weekend in question, Jenny was in a two sticks phase, finding life very difficult. A pastor-counsellor, an old friend of hers, came alongside her during what was a conference weekend and prepared her for prayer-ministry at the final Holy Communion Service. When the time came, I was privileged to make it a threesome. We began to pray for Jenny. When we asked the Lord to show us where the root of the disease lay, she began to tremble in a troubled way. We asked her what was happening, and she said 'I see a witch'. This was a totally unexpected development, a complete surprise to all three of us. My colleague then proceeded to lead Jenny through a process of renouncing all witchcraft in the Name of Jesus, and in that same Name, broke the hold of any curse which had passed on to her through her mother's or her father's bloodline. Jenny then went into a motionless trance-like but evidently peaceful state, remained so until well after the Service had finished, and then 'came to' and stood up. (She subsequently told us that she had had a marvellous sense of being on Father's knee in a state of total security). She walked out of the room unaided, and all I can tell you is that at the time of writing she has not had one symptom of the disease (which medically she still 'has') for three years. If that is spontaneous remission, then the Lord gave it, and praise be for His gift of spontaneous remission! I suppose that we might conceivably have asked her if she had had any dealings with the occult, but her answer would have been 'no'. We would have been stymied without the Lord's perception as well as helpless without His power to break a curse: Jenny would have been physically, mentally, emotionally and spiritually the poorer today.

B. From the Father, through The Son, by The Spirit – into our connecting

It was an inter-church celebration. There had been a time of worship, the good news had been splendidly proclaimed, and now there was a period of ministry as the Spirit of Christ moved upon the people, applying His goodness. A woman was crying and crying. One of my folk (let us call her Susan) moved to her: there was little time really, they had never met, and the cars and coaches were waiting. The problem was that the woman was quite unable to express her love for God or to receive love from Him, and yet the place was full of love. Susan could get no response from her beyond that, so asked the Lord for help: the Lord said 'she was sexually attacked when she was nine years old'. When the moment seemed right, Susan very gently interposed that and the woman was amazed: 'how did you know'? It was the necessary connection: the terrible secret had to be dealt with before she could love or be loved even by *the* Man. A few rows away sat another woman racked by sobbing and all scrunched up, so Susan next went to her and could get from her no indications whatever as to the cause of her distress. Susan checked with the Father Who said by His Spirit: 'she was sexually attacked when she was nine years old'. Susan explained politely to the Lord in her spirit that that was the message for the lady before! but the Lord said: 'Ask her'. Susan did. The woman was amazed: 'How did you know that?' It was the necessary connection: she, too, could not love 'Father', for her father had attacked her; that had to be dealt with first. I am perfectly well aware that sensitive counselling might well have uncovered the dark secret in each woman – it is not, alas! an uncommon scenario – but neither woman had been able to seek any such counselling. However, out of the compassion of His heart, the Father saw two of His daughters in deep distress, found another daughter who was prepared to listen to Him and sensitively to obey, and initiated the vital connection which had to be made between past and present. I wonder what are the mathematical odds for there being two women there both attacked at age 9, and Susan moving to precisely those two in a context of much ministering and many people? I cannot tell you what subsequently happened: I hope and trust that the two 'daughters' can now love and be loved by their Father.

C. From the Father, through the Son, by the Spirit – into our healing
Colin, as I shall call him, was a practising homosexual who was increasingly ill at ease about being a practising homosexual: he was finding it to be a rather wretched twilight existence, with the remains of his former Christian foundations putting pressure on his conscience. One of our lady counsellors (whom Colin had long known and respected) together with myself agreed to see him in a structured way over a period of some months. We were rather diffident, for he had already been through a course of sessions with a psychiatrist, he had acquainted himself with the work of Dr Moberly (see my summary in chapter 5) and had corresponded with her, and was generally more widely read and au fait with the subject than we were! Hardly surprisingly, after a few sessions only, we referred him on to a Christian counsellor who specialized in the subject, having experienced homosexual orientation himself but having decided as a Christian he could not and would not indulge in any sexual expression of it. A matter of weeks later, Colin was back with us! He had found the counsellor very genuine and helpful, he, Colin, had ceased from sexual activity, but somehow the thing was not yet 'cracked'. Subsequent sessions really went nowhere and then, one evening, Colin let us have it with both barrels, berating us, and in particular our God, for our joint abject failure to help him. It was a chastening experience. We duly crawled away to lick our wounds. As I reflected upon that experience, into my mind came the imagery of being pinned down in a trench while the enemy pounds your position with salvos of shells. 'Yes Lord, that is exactly how

it felt' was the gist of my response. 'No, no, I want you to shell *his* position with truth about Me' was the gist of His reply: I had to check that one out rather carefully because, in view of the week before, it was such an attractive proposition! In the event, I obeyed: I explained to Colin what I felt I should do, and did it. If I tell you that my heart was in my mouth, you will understand how my faith-level was at the time! But I did it: I fired a whole salvo from the Psalms. I used verses where the psalmists testify to the goodness and the power of God, as for example:

'But you are a shield around me, O Lord; you bestow glory on me and lift up my head' (Psalm 3.3);

'You hear, O Lord, the desire of the afflicted; you encourage them, and you listen to their cry' (Psalm 10.17);

'You O Lord, keep my lamp burning; my God turns my darkness into light. With your help I can run through a barricade; with my God I can scale a wall' (Psalm 18.28–29).

I produced a considerable salvo of that kind. I was amazed (that verb again!) at the result. Colin laid down his resistances like a lamb and began to open his heart to the Lord in a most moving way. That evening 'cracked' it. He was healed. Months later, he wrote to say that he was free from any homosexual desire or anxiety. Curiously, I am not sure that his Christian faith is yet rehabilitated and, if it is, he will certainly work it out in another fellowship than ours. The whole episode, though, says that the Lord has the perception and the power. Our weapon is 'the sword of the Spirit which is the Word of God' (Ephesians 6.17), surely a reference to the Word that the Lord speaks in, be it scripture or otherwise, to unlock a particular situation. It is not a matter of finding a Bible verse that seems to fit the bill: it is a matter of hearing God and being His mouth. I have no doubt whatever that my psalm sequence would roll off another counselee another day like water off a duck's back.

There are also particular areas of human difficulty where Christianity comes strongly into its own. I am thinking particularly of the problem of guilt associated with what is perceived to be terrible or even unforgivable sin, and of the privilege we have in leading counselees through to repentance and into forgiveness. I am assuming that readers of this book will be practised in that ministry, so I shall not elaborate. There is a good chapter on it entitled 'Repentance and Forgiveness', in Duncan Buchanan's book *The Counselling of Jesus*. What I would urge is that we remember the lesson of Mark 2.1–12: there are many, many people whose presenting problem may appear to have nothing to do with guilt or unforgivenness but whose real need is for forgiveness.

One other area of difficulty is when our counselling or prayer-ministry seems to provoke symptoms of demonic infestation in the counselee. In the days before spiritual renewal, I might have been reaching for some such phrase as dissociative hysterical neurosis if I had to, but when my teaching upon the reign of the Lord Jesus within us by the Spirit aroused in one young woman a very unholy spirit, and that evil thing looked at me and laughed, jeered, spat, played possum, pleaded and protested, the words 'demon' or 'unclean spirit' sufficed! I was petrified but the Lord was good. When that thing finally departed, the transformation in that young woman is one of my precious memories. My counsel would be that demons are only rarely encountered, although as the church bites into really pagan society, rather more may be dislodged from their hiding places; never go looking for demons – I fear that those who do are causing much damage to their 'victims'; never assume demonic presence until all other possible interpretations have been ruled out or the Lord gives you the discernment that an affliction is demonic; and when you know that it is, silence it, and drive it out in the Name of Jesus by the power of the Holy Spirit, *and* pray the Holy Spirit in. Spiritual renewal has aroused the demon-world: praise God that it gives the victory also!

Conclusions

What I have done in this chapter is to lay down the failures of the church and the victories of the Lord through His church side by side, really to remain there with each having its say and speaking its truth. The Hebrew mind, as I understand it, would have been content with that. We moderns would rather find a way to fuse the two together in one neat logical package. I cannot do that. Mercifully, I no longer feel a compulsion which demands that I try. At the end of the day, I encounter mystery. Here are two parallel counselling situations: the presenting problems have been explored, the connections have been made and understood, the underlying need has been laid bare, and the way in which Christ's Truth can meet the need is clear: there is an agreement in faith that what we pray for is a power-surge out of the heart of God to break the bondage and set the captive free, which is His royal prerogative. In the one instance, it happens: there is liberation, healing, hopefulness. In the other, it does not happen: there is deadlock, frustration, disappointment. It is all of a piece with people becoming Christians. I cannot make anyone a Christian, though goodness knows how hard I have sometimes tried. I can say all the right things, quote all the right promises and pray all the right prayers, but until there is that royal moment where a true yielding in repentance, need and faith is met by a new birthing act of God through His Son and by His Spirit, there will be no new Christian. So too in counselling. When nothing seems to happen, it is tempting to conjecture or pontificate, as some do, that there was not the faith, not the confidence that God's Word could accomplish the healing, not that yielding to His grace and power . . . Perhaps sometimes so . . . but the fact is that we just do not know, and we must accept the limitations of our own understanding *and* the limitlessness of God's sovereignty. My mind wanders to those situations in which we invested months and months of counselling in the Name of Jesus, and the counselees went away unhealed, some blessed and thankful, but one or two very angry. Why? We shall never know this side of eternity, and perhaps even the other side all we shall know is that it no longer matters to know. The activity of the Spirit of God is mysterious. All we can say with certainty is that God can and does change people but not in accordance with any formula we can concoct. The key verse of all in relation to spiritual renewal and all the Kingdom ministries is John 3.8:

'The wind blows wherever it pleases. You hear its sound,

but you cannot tell where it comes from or where it is going. So it is with everyone born of the Spirit.'

Section C

KEY PRACTICALITIES

7

Who is to counsel?

In the local church context, the counselling ideal is to develop a pool of able counsellors who work in close co-operation with the pastor and elders or church leaders. Such counsellors would come together to pray, share and learn, and, when the pastor passes over the name of a person needing counselling, would assign one or two of its number to make contact and arrange an initial interview with that person. The group would have, if possible, a living link with a professional or otherwise experienced Christian counsellor beyond its own fellowship, who can give a measure of supervision or direction to the group, or members of it, as required from time to time. The group would have and would wish to have a close working relationship with the pastor so that the church leadership is fully aware of the involvements the counselling group has at any given point in time: referrals to the group would normally come through the pastor or the elders' meeting, or, if people approached the counsellors directly, the counsellors would consult with the pastor before entering into any kind of commitment.

I am well aware that this ideal may seem to be completely beyond the reach of small fellowships whose committed nucleus members are already overstretched by too many church responsibilities. Nevertheless, it is good to have a goal to travel towards: to release one or two members into a counselling ministry could well be one of the Kingdom priorities a pastor has (see chapter 1 with its list of Kingdom priorities). The development of a small or larger team of counsellors does, however, raise issues of suitability, training, availability, supervision and the pastor's role.

The issue of suitability

Among the notes I have accumulated on aspects of counselling, I found one which I copied from I know not where which reads as follows:

I AM ALIVE	I AM DEAD
to the degree that I am –	to the degree that I am –
Aware: in touch with my feelings and with my body.	Out of touch with myself.
Relating: communicating with others in depth.	Living in the solitary confinement of a world of walls.
Authentic: open and congruent, owning myself.	*Phoney:* hidden, playing a cover-up role.
Caring: spontaneously caring and giving myself in relationships.	*Manipulating:* defensively controlling for egocentric ends.
Enjoying: pleasuring, playing, celebrating life.	*Plodding:* caught in the rat race I have created.
Spontaneous: free to experience and to choose.	*Compulsive:* programmed, driven by the oughts and shoulds.
Creating: making or doing something satisfying and/or significant.	*Vegetating:* treadmilling, engaged in unsatisfying and non-significant tasks.
Risking: adventuring.	*Playing it safe:* living in my box.
Present in the here-and-now, enriched by the past/future.	Existing in memories and future fantasies rather than in the present.

Coping responsibly with circumstances.	Being 'lived' by circumstances, blaming, projecting responsibility.
Connected with the Source – nature, the human race, God.	*Isolated:* 'an orphan' in the universe.
Growing towards using more of my potentialities.	Stagnating or regressing in the use of my gifts.

In those terms, we should be looking for men and women in our fellowship who are well on the way to being 'ALIVE'. No amount of counselling theory will compensate for a personality which is itself seriously immature or insecure. It would be extremely unwise to call a meeting 'for anyone who might be interested in training to be a counsellor': such an invitation may very well attract some who have powerful hidden agendas of their own, and who would be most unsuitable. That is not at all to suggest that anyone who has had difficulties with living is automatically disqualified, but it *is* to say that such a person should have worked through those difficulties and should have reached a place of solid emotional, mental and behavioural stability from which he can now reach out to others who are struggling.

It is also essential that would-be counsellors are possessed of a real measure of spiritual fitness and maturity. If we borrow Selwyn Hughes's Triad of *security, self-worth* and *significance* as being the deepest human needs and if we believe that it is only by knowing ourselves to be totally loved by God that those clamant needs can be met, then it is axiomatic that suitable counsellors are they who have themselves found their own security, self-worth and significance in living relationship with God: they are receiving what they themselves need from the Father, through the Son, by the Spirit. They know that the divine 'I love you' means 'I am with you always' which is their security, means 'you are precious in my sight' which gives them their self-worth, and means 'you are my beloved son, daughter' which gives them their significance. Furthermore, as in the current renewal we discover how dependence upon the Spirit releases the resources of the Father and the Son into the here and now to meet human needs, so it is crucial that counsellors are as their Master and His followers in the New Testament testimony: all we need do to catch the essence is to note the telling descriptive clauses:

Peter, of Jesus: 'anointed with the Holy Spirit and power' (Acts 10.38).

John, of Jesus: 'full of grace and truth' (John 1.14).

Mark, of Jesus: 'filled with compassion' (Mark 1.41).

Luke, of Jesus: 'full of joy through the Holy Spirit' (Luke 10.21).

In Acts, the Apostles say of new leaders to be appointed:

'Choose men from among you who are known to be full of the Spirit and wisdom' (Acts 6.3).

Of Stephen, it is written:

'A man full of faith and of the Holy Spirit' (Acts 6.5)

and

'A man full of God's grace and power' (Acts 6.8).

Of Peter and of Paul it says:

'Then, filled with the Holy Spirit, he . . .'. (e.g. Acts 4.8 and 13.9).

Of Barnabas, it stands written:

'full of the Holy Spirit and faith' (Acts 11.24).

Something of the very *life* and *personality* of the Lord needs to be astir within the Christian counsellor.

Whilst on the matter of suitability and fitness, I am increasingly convinced that frontline Christian workers need 'sabbaticals', periods of resting and refreshment. This holds good for busy counsellors who may, in any case, come up against crises of their own and need their own space and time to work such things through. This is one of the several reasons why I believe that it is often good for our local church counsellors to work in pairs: that way, there is support and cover if the one counsellor needs a break. Too many of our nucleus church workers suffer from a process of spiritual burn-out to the point where the Spirit no longer superintends or empowers their work. Counselling *costs* the counsellor: counsellors need to be fairly fit physically, emotionally, intellectually and spiritually; to maintain their fitness, they may sometimes need to remain in the team but to have a break from counselling responsibility itself.

The issue of training

I would hope that it is already clear from previous chapters that training for counsellors is a must. There are certainly people who have a natural aptitude for caring and being understanding, but there are aspects of counselling which can only be learned and others which can certainly be improved by the disciplines of study and group exploration. Counsellors need to understand the counselling relationship itself which is crucial to the whole process of healing and has its own very special dynamics; they need to acquire the ability to read the script of what is actually going on, for instance, in terms of transference or even counter-transference; they need to be thoroughly acquainted with the skills required to enable the processes of exploring, connecting and healing (see chapter 5) to take place as deeply as is required; and, witness my own indebtedness in respect of exploring more deeply the dynamics of depression or of homosexual orientation (see chapter 5), they need to be familiar with the anatomy of depression or grief or guilt or whatever, for which purposes much material is available which it would be foolish to ignore.

What kind of training is to be recommended? Personally I have encouraged the counsellors in my fellowship to go for the best of three worlds! Firstly, to enrol in a group embarking on a pastoral counselling course run by the Westminster Pastoral Foundation (you can enrol for one, two or three years and go on to do supervised counselling work for the

Foundation): the strength of such a course is that it draws primarily upon professional expertise whether secular or Christian, so that its students acquire a good number of tools, and it is strong in role-play, workshop practice and supervision, so that the students are themselves opened up emotionally and mentally. However, the assumed theological framework would be too liberal for many of us (see Roger Hurding's balanced critique of the W.P.F. in his 'Roots and Shoots', Chapter 10). Accordingly, secondly, let counsellors take advantage also of the counselling seminars made available by the Crusade for World Revival and led by Selwyn Hughes. These seminars are not as exhaustive or sustained as the W.P.F. ones, but their strength is that, although they draw on secular expertise, the whole cast of counselling is much more securely founded upon the revelation of Scripture and is more unabashedly Christian: Jesus Christ is held to be the Way, the Truth and the Life which all men and women most truly need and seek. Thirdly, all my counsellors have attended conferences led by John Wimber and his Vineyard Pastors, principally to learn about prayer-ministry in the power of the Holy Spirit. In what John Wimber calls 'clinic', participants are encouraged to minister to one another, expecting that the Holy Spirit will bestow His gifts upon them as they do, and will move powerfully to heal at various levels: in his healing seminars, John Wimber recognizes that the human being is a complex entity and that there are different levels and dimensions of healing, often inter-related: for example, the healing of the Spirit (that is the renewal and restoration of relationship with God), of past hurts, of the body, of relationships, and healing from demonic bondage. Since those healing areas represent a considerable overlap with those for counselling, our counsellors need to learn to be open to the Lord to discern when the time may be right for prayer-ministry to a counselee in the power of the Holy Spirit. I am fortunate indeed to have several counsellors now who have been through the three kinds of training: add the ongoing stimulus of meeting together or in pairs and of attending occasional counselling conferences or workshops such as are now widely available, and you have a counselling team with strong foundations.

The issue of availability

Sheer busyness seems to be one of the debilitating afflictions of our age in general and of committed Christians in particular. Pastors (who are generally perceived to be too busy and who very often themselves talk the language of being too busy) have to live with the guilt of seeming so often to be placing yet more demands upon already over-committed Christians. In this matter also we need to have a goal: full-time leaders apart, I advocate that our members be involved in Sunday Worship, one weekly cell meeting, plus a ministry in one of the Kingdom Priority areas: evangelism and community involvement, prayer and worship, teaching and discipling, healing and pastoral care, or in the support ministries of administration or leadership. I long to see a strong team established to head up the mission ministry in each of these priority areas. I should hasten to add that the fellowship I lead is a long way from achieving that but it is a mark towards which we press. This means that our counsellors should be otherwise released from church involvements, although I realize how difficult that is in practice to achieve. I have the tremendous boon of four counsellors who are not in employment and whose lives, therefore, have at any rate a degree of elasticity which permits them to do much pastoral care and some counselling. On the other hand, all of my present team of counsellors are women: I do not have any men who have been able to go through the three-tier training schedule I outlined earlier in this chapter. Where a counselling situation calls for the involvement of a man, I generally have to be that man: our cell leaders would certainly be able to exercise general pastoral care, but they would not generally have the time or expertise to be involved in structured ongoing counselling. There is no answer to these time-and-opportunity difficulties: we have to live with the tensions and frustrations of them but resolutely head in the direction of releasing some of our people into counselling and of building a team whilst living within the parameters imposed upon us: we should take on only those counselees to whom we can offer the time and energy they need.

The issue of supervision

In the current practice of the afore-mentioned Westminster Pastoral Foundation, a trainee counsellor, following three years of training, is assigned to a small group of practising counsellors which meets for a one-and-a-half hour session weekly under the supervision of a highly experienced practitioner: the group members are thus able to share what is happening in the counselling relationships in which they are currently involved and to open their counselling to the experience and insight of the group, as well as to discuss carefully who should take on which of the new clients who have been accepted for counselling. Some supervisory facility is available to all counsellors, even if they are greatly experienced. Surely there needs to be at least some equivalent for those who counsel within the aegis of the local church. 'Supervision' should be viewed very positively: it is *for the good of the counsellor* (and therefore of the counselee) that it should be in place in some form. It may be that a church counsellor can look to a professional or more experienced counsellor for guidance and direction. It may be that the pastor or pastoral elder needs to sit down with each church counsellor from time to time, and it is of benefit to both counsellor and counselee if the former has the prior permission of the latter (within agreed limits of confidentiality) to share with the pastor, pastoral elder or supervisor. Working in pairs, with the one taking the lead, has the advantage of enabling the other to monitor and reflect upon the style and progress of the initiator. If there is a counselling group, then one of the functions of the group is to enable any member to draw inspiration or encouragement from the others and, indeed, to offload any hurt feelings or joyous ones. The group can also tackle complex issues together, thereby opening up the inner attitudes its members may have, and exposing those to the wisdom of the others and to the light of the Scriptures: for example, our church group has tackled the counselling issues relative to people who know they are H.I.V. positive or who are actually dying from A.I.D.S.; it is important to check our own feelings and thoughts on such issues upon the sounding-board of a group of Christian friends and fellow-counsellors. Churches too often fall to the temptation of letting the committed get on with the ministry they have chosen without getting alongside them to check how they are doing and how they are feeling about their ministry: many of the workers in church organizations feel an acute sense of isolation because the church at large does not *seem* to care. It would be both unwise and unfair to allow a church counsellor to sink or swim on his own month after month.

The issue of the pastor's role

The Holy Spirit has revivified the New Testament concept of the church as the Body of Christ, with each member a living part of it: we are rediscovering the living meaning of our own jargon! 'Member' means 'limb', an actively working part of the Body. Each Christian has a ministry in the Body and his ministry is essential to the overall efficiency of the Body. This has been widely taught: it has often been backed up by gift-discovery exercises or questionnaires, but, in too many instances, local fellowships have failed to release their members into the ministries they have discovered they ought to have! Some kind of grid is required: the one I have stayed with in this book is that of Kingdom Ministries or Priorities, being evangelism and community involvement, prayer and worship, teaching and discipling, and healing and pastoral care, girt about with ministries of Leadership and Administration. In New Testament principle, then, each Christian will have a particular ministry in one of those areas. So, for example, those whose gifts are of the encouraging, caring and serving ilk will find their ministry within the healing and pastoral care Kingdom priority and, out of their number, will emerge the counsellors-to-be. It is the pastor's role, in conjunction with the other leaders of the church, to release people into their ministries. What does that entail? It includes constantly feeding in creative and Biblical ideas as to *how* to fulfil a ministry of prayer or evangelism or teaching or caring. Not everyone can have a church 'job' – that is, a clearly defined slot within the organized structure of the local church, like a treasurer or door steward or Sunday School teacher (although so many churches have a struggle merely to fill those posts); some Kingdom priorities cannot be structured in that sort of way: for instance, caring cannot be *organized* in a regimented way but church leaders can suggest what such a ministry of caring might work out at, and can encourage the carers to take caring initiatives in and out from their cell, for example, or amongst the younger or the older, and so forth. The pastor needs to ensure that guidelines are being supplied – most people are slow to initiate, so someone needs to create the environment, space or motivation for them to make a move – and that there are opportunities for ministries to be embarked upon and fulfilled. At the same time, the pastor also needs to be helping his members to find out who they are in the Body, and/or to be helping them on into larger ministries. In relation to counselling, it is the pastor's responsibility (listening, of course, to what others in the fellowship are saying) to discern, select, encourage and spiritually direct those who have the gifting for the ministry of counselling. That will include seeking to ensure that they are suitably trained.

There is a very real and pressing issue here. This may be controversial, but my sense is that it may be more important for the pastor to release the right members into counselling than for him to give his own energies to counselling, or into evangelizing than for him to be the evangelist, or into discipling than for him to try to do it all, or into leading worship than for him always to lead it. It can never be a totally tidy either/or, and clearly is not so in the ministry of Jesus, but Jesus evidently did put a lot of time and energy into enabling his committed followers to continue His mission-ministry. Pastors who feel that they have a specialist ministry in one of the Kingdom priority areas, say, that of evangelizing or counselling or teaching, and who devote themselves to that particular ministry, very often find themselves led down a road which takes them out of the local church pastorate and into some translocal specialist ministry. The local church pastor is more the enabler than the specialist and I believe he should rejoice in the privilege of that. Most of my counsellors are now better *trained* than I am, though I have some years of experience in hand still! They will increasingly move alongside people in deep need whom I could not reach or give myself to, and in that I rejoice. The considerable time I have invested in encouraging counsellors is reaping richer dividends for the Kingdom than if I had bowed to the assumption that the pastor has to do whatever counselling is done in the local fellowship.

In conclusion, let me stress that it is good all round if the counsellors maintain living links with the pastor and eldership. It is also good that when, along the counselling way, a point of significant prayer-ministry is called for, the counsellor enlists the help of the pastor (or appropriate leader) for that specific purpose. This presupposes, of course, that the counselee knows that that is how the counselling system works, and has given assent for the measure of sharing that would be necessary. Rather like the altars of stones the Old Testament patriarchs built as memorials to moments when they encountered the Living God, these prayer points can stand as important landmarks along the road to greater wholeness, and it is good, probably for all concerned, for a church leader to be associated with the counsellor in enabling a counselee to receive good things from the Father through the Son by the Spirit. My elders and I would always endeavour to make ourselves available, and gladly so, in such circumstances.

8

Who is to be counselled?

I have a dream: in my dream, a man makes contact with me saying that his life is in trouble and he would like to share some things with me. We arrange a first meeting at which he outlines the contours of his situation, let us say a marriage which is increasingly characterized by tension and open conflict. I suggest a way ahead, given that there is the desire and will to save and repair this marriage, namely, that one of our women counsellors, let us call her Ruth, sits down with his wife, woman to woman, and I sit down with him, man to man, to explore the causes and then the roots of the conflict between them, with their joint agreement that Ruth and I may share one with the other anything they say apart from information which either expressly forbids us to repeat. Ruth then sits down with the wife and I with the husband, and each is willing and co-operative in the exploratory stages: there is good ventilation of pent-up feelings, there is a deal of personal honesty, and a good amount of resolve to build a better marriage for the future. Ruth and I consult and put it to the couple that it is time for our twosomes to become a foursome since there are things which each needs to hear the other say, there are some past events to be jointly surveyed and dealt with, there needs to be a re-capitulation and mutual avowal of the causes and roots of their difficulties, and there will need to be formulated a plan of action in the form of agreed manageable steps towards healing and progress. They agree, and all of that is done in a foursome. The couple accept agreed 'homework', the challenge and opportunity of jointly agreed 'tasks', and subsequent foursomes yield evidence of hopeful gains. All four of us starting out from a Christian base, we are also able to look to and utilize the resources of God's love to undergird this journey into better days. The couple plan a holiday away where they will be together all day every day and we work through both the opportunity and the threat of that, as a result of which their holiday is a considerable success which encourages them and us. There comes the day when they tell Ruth and me that they no longer need to see us on an ongoing basis but will stay in touch.

That is, albeit in shorthand, any counsellor's dream: the ideal of counselees who are wanting and able to be co-operative, are open and honest, agree a modus operandi, work hard, take on homework tasks, and make real progress. Those are the kind of people who should be counselled! Unfortunately, I have discovered that the dream regularly becomes reality only in the testimonies of other people's books on counselling, rather as Adrian Plass discovered in relation to evangelism: he read a book on street evangelism in which crowds of people always flocked eagerly to the evangelist and were always converted like meek little lambs; I fully identify with Adrian's discovery within himself of a desire to kick the author between miracles! I cast my dream in a form relating to marital conflict and its resolution principally because something of the sort did happen in my experience of counselling: it all went *too much* like the textbooks say and as in my dream but even then I was beguiled. A matter of weeks after the couple had dispensed with our services, the one partner abruptly left the supposedly reconstructed marital nest in order to live with a paramour, and the marriage was finally destroyed. So beware of the ideal counselling paradigm! However, what the dream does throw into relief, made sharper still by the subsequent catastrophe in reality, are the basic issues relating to who is to be counselled and, by implication, who is not.

The issue of the agenda

Too much of what is called 'counselling' in the local church suffers from being ill-defined, indisciplined and inadequate, as well as being adversely affected by the tyranny of the urgent. Pastors, pastoral leaders, counsellors or whoever is being looked to for care and counselling need to learn not to be afraid of being straightforward and, to a degree, businesslike in their dealings with those who head in their direction with personal difficulties. I am, of course, speaking of a firmness which is *warm*. To begin with, when an arrangement is made, it should be clear: the date, the time, the place, the duration and the purpose should be up front so that counsellor and counselee have a clear understanding of basics from the start; many Christian counsellors shy away from seeming to be 'professional' or briskly efficient, but why? A clear basis for the relationship is a positive aid to the counselee. Furthermore, the pastoral counsellor needs to shoulder his responsibility of determining on the basis of the initial interview or one or two subsequent sessions what the appropriate kind of help is. There is now so much Christian literature concerning types of Biblical counselling, the healing of memories, deliverance from the demonic, inner healing and the like, that there is developing an *assumption* that whenever people admit to a problem with life, we must immediately dig deeply into their early life experiences and stored emotions, and open a can of worms. This is a quite improper assumption, which, if followed automatically, may well leave a lot of people damaged and disappointed. It is also a dangerous assumption since over-preoccupation with, or the exalting of, counselling can – by a process akin to auto-suggestion – *produce* more and more of the very conditions it is supposed to heal. What all counselling figures need to understand is that a range of options is available to us when people bring their difficulties to us, and it is our responsibility to decide upon the pastoral response to be made. A good wrestle with Howard Clinebell's *Basic Types of Pastoral Care and Counselling* will help counsellors come to terms with the decision to be made. For example, a high percentage of those who come to us come in current crisis: life has thrown up a problem which the person is finding to be too difficult for his usual problem-coping or problem-solving abilities. What the majority require is not formally structured ongoing in-depth counselling, but someone who will stand alongside for a while, who listens, who cares, who offers warmth, meaning and hope and, if need be, practical support. Indeed, Clinebell would argue that the major contribution of pastors and churches to people in trouble is likely to be this that he calls 'supportive care and counselling' rather than 'uncovering pastoral psychotherapy'.

Supportive counselling care aims to enable people to come to terms with their problems, relationships and circumstances in a more constructive and fruitful manner within the limits set by their own personality capabilities and life situation. The care-counsellor will offer reassurance, encouragement, guidance, practical suggestions or resources, rather than initiating moves to probe, uncover and confront. Such ministry gives 'good counsel', but it will be given for a *limited* period of time, being further sustained by occasional contacts and brief counselling sessions as and when required. What all of this says is that if and when the counsellor decides upon uncovering counselling as the required agenda, he does need to be sure that it is a journey which the counselee needs and is at least to a degree willing and able to make, and which he, the counsellor, is competent and able to make. It is true that we Christians find it hard to say no, because to do so seems to imply rejecting people or letting them down or denying our message that Jesus Christ is the Way, the Truth and the Life, and all of that makes us feel guilty. However, hard though it is, I have learned to say within myself: 'no, I will not undertake the uncovering journey with you, even though you are making signals that I should do so; I will give you first-aid care now, I will pray with you and for you, I will provide supportive care for you through this fellowship; I will also refer you to someone more experienced and expert than I, if that seems right to me and is acceptable to you, but no, I will not make the inward and downward journey with you, because I discern, I *know*, that so to commit myself would take me way beyond my competence and my present knowledge and/or I see that you do not have the personal resources and/or you do not have the intention or the will to make that journey'. The subject matter may be set by the person who presents his difficulties to us but it is we who must shape the agenda for responding appropriately. It is we who decide who is to be counselled in the longer-term meaning of that word.

By way of a brief postscript to this section, I should add that

I would not encourage local church carers and counsellors to become deeply involved with persons clearly suffering from serious personality disorders or from major psychotic difficulties such as schizophrenia or paranoia. We should certainly offer such persons genuine and compassionate care whilst recognizing that if they are to be significantly helped, professional expertise will be required. On the vexed question of psychiatric methods, I would recommend that counsellors read and ponder, for example, Dr David Enoch's book *Healing the Hurt Mind* (Hodder and Stoughton, 1983), and particularly his spirited and informed defence of the use of antipsychotic, antidepressant and antitension drugs, Dr Enoch being both a leading psychiatrist and a committed Christian.

The issue of confidentiality

Our first thought may be to wonder how confidentiality can be an issue at all. Surely all that passes between counselee and counsellor is strictly confidential by definition and that is the end of the matter? Not necessarily. In the dream with which this chapter began, you will have noted that both the husband and wife gave permission to Ruth and me to share what each said to either of us, unless there was any particular information which the one or the other did not want shared at all. As I have indicated in the previous chapter, I believe there can be real gain for two counsellors to share with a counselee if the latter has no objection or difficulty with that: the sharing and reflecting of counsellors together can be very productive as to the future direction of the counselling and is therefore of benefit to all concerned. I have also indicated that there may be a point of prayer-ministry at which it is good to bring in the pastor or one of the church leaders to aid and abet the healing-process, and in those circumstances too, a measure of sharing is beneficial. If a counsellor has a supervisor or director, it is good to have counselees' permission to share at least the anatomy of the difficulty being explored, even if no identities are necessarily divulged. So it is as well to discuss the boundaries of confidentiality with a counselee at an early point in the proceedings: the golden rule is then that agreed boundaries may not be exceeded without the express permission of the counselee.

There is, however, another aspect to confidentiality within the context of a local church fellowship. This was brought home to me by contact with a fellowship in which much damage was done under the guise of 'confidentiality'. In that fellowship, a particular person, operating out of a deep anger which she denied, went to this and that person in the fellowship, pouring out a catalogue of complaint against the church leaders, and making allegations, but binding each person to secrecy. She also wrote long letters to other people, but again, always 'in strictest confidence'. In this way, confidentiality actually became a weapon of manipulation, a force for evil and not for good. What I am suggesting here is that in the local church context, there can be counselling situations where absolute confidentiality is used to tie the counsellor's hands behind his back, so preventing other resources from being harnessed. Sometimes, therefore, when a person indicates that he has something to share 'in strictest confidence', it becomes necessary and/or is illuminating to explore *first* why the something can only be shared 'in the strictest confidence': what is the real point and purpose of the condition of confidentiality?

In view of the content of the two paragraphs above, I at least raise the issue as to whether there might be circumstances in which we would decline to counsel persons who will not permit us to share anything at all with anyone else under any circumstances.

The issue of time

The processes of a therapeutic counselling relationship which I outlined in chapter 5 as being those of exploring, connecting and healing all require *time*. Very substantial personal difficulties which took years in the making are not about to clear themselves up in five minutes. It is therefore of the essence that if we commit ourselves to formal counselling, we are committed for as long as the journey takes. It follows that those of us in local churches who have other functions to fulfil within the Body should take on for counselling only those persons to whom we can give the unpressured time required. Given that they will also be involved in some one-off first-aid care sessions, and in a measure of supportive care work at any given period of time, I would think it unlikely that pastors or lay counsellors could also cope with more than three ongoing counselling relationships at any one time, even allowing that counselling sessions will be limited to within one and a half hours each. Availability of time and at the times required does have a bearing on who can be counselled and when.

The issue of genders

In the context of the local church setting, should a man invariably be counselled by a man or men and a woman by a woman or women? It is rather like one of those questions put to Paul by the Christians in Corinth where one has to say: 'I have no commandment from the Lord, but here is my own best wisdom' (c.f.I Corinthians 7.25). I do not believe that there is an inviolable law on the matter, but the issue does require some honesty and wisdom because ministries and marriages have been destroyed by emotional, and then sexual, entanglements which began innocently as man counselling woman or vice versa. Counsellors should be in sufficiently good touch with their own feelings to be able to read the writing on the wall from a good distance and take appropriate defensive or evasive action. However, in the learning stages, counsellors can become too emotionally involved with a counselee before realizing it: moreover, I doubt if I am the only pastor who, in the midst of many pressures and grumbles, can find it rather refreshing and flattering to be regarded by an attractive woman as being the best thing since sliced bread, even if I know very well that this is a temporary transference of affection away from her husband who is not currently deemed worthy to receive it! On bad days, this can be a dangerous scenario. Accordingly, I again point out the advantages of having pairs of counsellors (a man and woman working in tandem can be very strong), particularly in the case of inexperienced counsellors. Where in smaller fellowships there simply is not the luxury of choice, the wisest course is man to man and woman to woman; where that is not possible, the counsellor does need to take the potential difficulties seriously, particularly where the nature of the presenting problem is that of marital conflict or sexual frustration. As one who has been (falsely) accused of having an affair with a counselee, I remind pastors that they need not only to be above suspicion but, as far as possible, to be *seen* to be above suspicion. If in doubt, do not counsel someone of the opposite sex alone: if you find yourself becoming enmeshed and are afraid you cannot cope with it, get someone else in or get yourself out.

The issue of taking the initiative

Do we only ever counsel those who come to us? or do we also look out for those who need help but feel unable to come and ask for it? I think we must opt for the latter because Jesus Himself did. Goodness knows that more than enough people presented their needs to Him, yet the fact remains that He went to Zacchaeus and to the Samaritan woman at the well to initiate saving and healing relationship with them which they were totally unable to initiate themselves – indeed, that in itself was part of their problem. So we do need to be sensitive as to how people are and to move alongside the troubled in order that they are given an opportunity to find help. There is, however, another aspect to taking the initiative which is more specifically applicable to local fellowships of Christians than to anywhere else: I would call it 'Preventive Care Counselling', and it becomes possible particularly at the great moments of life for which the church has the privilege of providing the preparation. Let me instance two in particular: those of preparation for marriage, and preparation (in our case) for believers' Baptism and church membership.

Everyone acknowledges that we have a modern marriage crisis in our western world. The statistics for divorce each year are appalling, being in this country of the order of one in three first marriages ending in divorce, the true situation in terms of human misery being bound to be worse than the statistics. Half a million men, women and children are being caught up in the trauma of family break-up each year in our society. But why? The major reason has to be that the expectations of husbands and/or wives are simply not being attained. Confirmation of that came from a television study of modern marriage in different cultures. One of the findings was that, overall, Indian wives were slightly more satisfied with their married lot than their North American counter-parts. When you compare the lifestyles of the two groups, that is a truly astonishing finding, particularly if, as I have, you have been to India and seen the lot of many married women there at first hand. What the finding surely says is that there is a world of difference between the marriage expectation of North American as distinct from Indian women, and that the expectations of the Indian women are more earthed in reality and are therefore more attainable than those of North American wives. Does this not therefore strongly suggest that we in the churches should do some substantial work with couples who come to us for marriage, particularly in the area of their expectations and their values as they approach marriage? This will not be *called* 'coun-selling' of course, but surely that is what it is? In our fellow-ship, we have encouraged one of our own couples who have successfully managed important adjustments in their own marriage to develop such a ministry in marriage preparation. Furthermore, a while ago, that couple plus my wife and I spent half a day with six young couples who had been prepared for marriage and married in our church during the previous year, and we encouraged those couples to share and reflect upon the quality and relevance of our preparation, and upon how they were faring as young married couples. Quite clearly, marriage had brought its share of surprises and equally clearly, there were expectation adjustments and priority adjustments needing to be worked through. Signifi-cantly, despite natural initial reticence, the couples concerned voted the occasion a great encouragement to them, some being almost visibly relieved to note that other newly-weds were facing similar adjustments to their own. I call that preventive care counselling which is worthy of our top quality resources.

There is also the decisive Christian event of conversion and initiation into the Body of Christ and into the local expression of it. It seems to me that the preparation and early nurture of new Christians is a major opportunity for preventive care counselling. On the one hand, it is the time to lay the foun-dation of a 'now' and 'not yet' Kingdom Discipleship: as we have seen, there is a great Christian 'now' and we should teach it and lead new Christians into it, but, as John Bunyan has immortally depicted, they will not spend all their time by the River of the Water of Life or on the Delectable Mountains. They will also be called upon to withstand the trials and tribulations of the Hill called Difficulty, the Valley of Humiliation where Apollyon (the destroyer or the devil) attacks, Vanity Fair, By-path Meadow and Doubting Castle, before the marvellous 'not yet' of the Celestial City. Furthermore, taking a different perspective from that of John Bunyan, the local company of Christians, albeit born again and Spirit-filled, alternately delights and infuriates, excites and deflates, leads you to the gates of paradise and drives you to distraction! Sometimes within that company, the sheep give a very convincing imitation of goats, and your eyes see couch-grass rather than wheat! We need to help new Christians to make the transition there *is* from the exhiliaration of their being cleansed, saved, liberated and filled with the Spirit, to the sturdy peace and inner conviction of daily discipleship rooted and grounded in Christ as He is *and* earthed in the relationships, circumstances and events of daily life as it is. This is crucial work: too many new Christians are still falling away and off the edges of the churches, their unreal, unbiblical expectation being unchecked and thus unrealized. The care crucially needed is in the period before and after Christian initiation, and the twin poles to be pointed to are the 'now' and the 'not yet'. I have set out the importance of this foundational Kingdom understanding in chapter 2 and need not elaborate further. On the other hand however, here is also the opportunity to lay the ghosts of the past. In our fellowship, we have evolved a pre-baptismal ceremony as a landmark point of baptismal preparation. The Baptisands gather with the church leaders a day or two before their baptism and are encouraged to visualize the Lord standing there before them with an open Wheelie Bin! Into that bin, they are to place anything and everything from their past which is undealt with or which might hinder a free and full flow of relating with Christ the Lord; we invite the Holy Spirit to locate anything that remains and to enable the person to throw that anything into the bin, to let go of it and let Jesus wheel it away to its destruction: the sins, the shame, the trauma, the secret things, the suppressed feelings, whatever . . . Some such thing was an instinct the Spirit prompted from the start, for in ancient church liturgies, there was provision for exorcism before baptism. The rubbish-bin imagery is natural enough, and we subsequently discovered that Pastor John Bedford who ministers from a Birmingham base has worked with that imagery to a more advanced degree than we have. Each new Christian in his fellowship works his or her way through 'The Dustbin Sheet'. Let us suppose that Theresa has committed her life to Christ and is approaching Baptism: she is given the Dustbin Sheet and is encouraged to follow through what it says. The Sheet encourages her to spend an hour or two recalling and writing down all matters about which she discovers she still has *feelings* of guilt, whether matters of commission or omission. Theresa is then encouraged to receive and to know God's forgiveness, and to thank Him and love Him for His Grace towards her. Then, across the reverse of the paper, she writes:

> 'If we confess our sins, he is faithful and just and will forgive us our sins and purify us from all unrighteousness' (1 John 1.9).

Theresa signs the paper as her written confession and then BURNS it. She is further exhorted by the Dustbin Sheet to find another hour or two to make a list of all the things from the past which still *hurt* and make her feel angry or resentful. She asks forgiveness for hanging onto grievance, and she forgives the person who caused each hurt. She writes across the back of that paper:

> 'Be kind and compassionate to one another, forgiving each other, just as in Christ God forgave you' (Ephesians 4.32).

Theresa then signs and BURNS that paper also. The way is now clear for the declaration of baptism and for full and free relating with her Lord through the moving of the Holy Spirit within her. It should be added that during this whole process, an experienced Christian counsellor is available to her at any point where she knows she needs help. I commend this method to you as an excellent example of taking the initiative at a crucial point along life's way, so that a great deal of material in our personal histories which has been buried alive is dealt with in the name of Christ so that it cannot rise up to devour us later on.

9

The how, when, where, and until of counselling

Brother, let me be your servant,
Let me be as Christ to you;
Pray that I may have the grace
To let you be my servant, too.

We are pilgrims on a journey,
We are brothers on the road;
We are here to help each other
Walk the mile and bear the load.

I will hold the Christ-light for you
In the night-time of your fear;
I will hold my hand out to you,
Speak the peace you long to hear.

I will weep when you are weeping;
When you laugh I'll laugh with you.
I will share your joy and sorrow
'Til we've seen this journey through.

When we sing to God in Heaven
We shall find such harmony,
Born of all we've known together
Of Christ's love and agony.

Richard Gillard (Thank you Music).

Although this song has not found a place for itself in the

charismatic hit-parade, there are few others which as potently convey what Christians should be to one another in Christ. This is a song to be sung to one another – and in the form 'sister, let me be your servant,' too. This book has already argued that one of the messages of the Spirit to the churches is that we Christians should take our relationships with one another far more seriously. One particular form of such deep relating is that relationship in which a counsellor is saying to a counselee 'let me be as Christ to you'. How can that be? and when? and where? and until?

The question of how

In this chapter, we shall suppose that 'Martha' has come to you looking for your help. You have had an initial session or two with her. Your genuine warmth and your developed skill of giving yourself to listening and to accurate reflecting back to her of the feelings she is trying to put into words have encouraged her to risk ventilating some deep-down bottled-up emotions; meanwhile, you have gained a tentative initial impression of how life looks from within her world, of how she views the problem presented, and of the resources she may have of coming to terms with the underneath of her difficulties. Let us suppose that your perception is that you do not need at this juncture to refer her to some specialist agency but rather that you should and are able to offer her continuing counselling. How do you proceed?

There is an initial nitty-gritty 'how', and that is to establish mutual agreement between Martha and yourself as to the basis on which you will make the counselling journey together. To that end, you agree with Martha that you will see her normally on a weekly basis for an hour's session and will continue to do so providing that both of you sense that progress is being made; if you feel that a second counsellor could fruitfully be involved or if you will wish to share something of this relationship with your pastor, perhaps with a view to joint prayer-ministry at a later stage, then you will seek Martha's assent to that; you indicate to Martha that, because you believe in a team approach to human difficulties, if along the way you feel that some specialist help may be needed, you would put that to her for her agreement; you mention that manageable assignments may prove to be a helpful part of the process; and, of course, you arrange the date, time and place of your next meeting together. In this way, Martha has the security of knowing where she is with you and of knowing a little about the way you work and about what she may expect, whereas at the same time you have the security of having an agreed framework for the counselling process. The rest of the counselling 'how' relates to how you make real progress towards journey's end. The way is known to you in that it is to be an adventure of exploring, connecting and healing; you have your resources human and divine as per chapters 4, 5 and 6 of this book, being your church fellowship, your counselling tools, and the power of the Spirit of the Sovereign Lord; and the markers of progress are familiar to you in that you will be looking for constructive change in the presenting problem itself, for signs of positive behavioural and relational strides being taken, for indicators of genuine self-insight gains, and for the emergence of a Martha who abides in Jesus Christ as her living Saviour and Lord, who knows in her inmost being that she is unconditionally loved, valued and accepted by Him and that she is responsible to Him for her actions and reactions. So then, how is progress to be made along that royal road? It is true that there are many models of counselling methodology, and each with its own emphasis, but it is difficult to see how the efficacy of any of them can depend at root on other than the quality of the counselling relationship itself. Such a conclusion should be no surprise either, for, after all, so much of who and how we are derives from the quality of our primary relationship with our mother and father right from the beginning of our life. Furthermore, Christians know very well that the living heart of the Gospel's power to change people is *relationship* with the Lord: through Jesus Christ, and Him crucified and risen, we can have real relationship with God; it is that relationship itself which is the catalyst for our being cleansed and made new and for our continuing to be renewed. In both the making of us vis-à-vis our parents and the re-making of us vis-à-vis our God, the crucial agency is the quality of the relationship. That truth holds good for the ministry of counselling. Evelyn Peterson in her book *Who Cares?* makes the powerful point that, just as it is true that

Martha's perception of reality and the consequent conclusions she drew about life and living derived initially from her relationship with her parents *then*, so it *remains* true that relationship is the key to her perceptions of reality and her convictions about life and living *now*. If the first relationship was deficient in love and dependability, leading to a distorted view of the world and to confused convictions about living, a subsequent relationship which is rich in love and dependability can lead to a more hopeful view of the world and a more mature comprehension of what life is about and how it is best to be lived. The counselling relationship itself may very well be that subsequent relationship; if it cannot be, little progress may be made, but if it can, and, more, if, because we are dealing with counselling in a Christian context, that counselling relationship has the rich inlay of relationship with Christ, then substantial change and growth towards His stature become possible.

Suppose that Martha's root problem is one of rejection: a damaging relationship with her father gave her a view of reality as inconsistent and hostile, instilling within her what is now her 'truth' that at the end of the day she is unlovable and everyone will and does reject her (a script which her behaviour will often work to bring about and thus justify her 'truth'). It is of minimal value merely to enable her to read and understand that scenario: after all, what does that change? It does not necessarily help either to lay before her Scriptures which show clearly that 'the Lord loves you, Martha, and accepts you and always will'; she may well reply 'yes I know that – with my head; but my heart doesn't know it'. She needs more than explanations and scriptures. What needs to happen for her is that in the relationship with you, you *are* accepting love; you *convey* acceptance and steadfastness; to some real degree, you *are* the love which Christ is, that love which forgives, shares and encourages (see chapter 4). In that way, through relationship with you, Christ communicates and conveys his love to Martha, drawing her towards *experiencing* the love that will not let her go: as that happens, she revises her view of reality and her convictions about life. Such counselling is both high privilege and awesome responsibility. From time to time, all of us counsellors need jolting back into conscious awareness of both those aspects.

Having made mention of that rich inlay of relationship with Christ which gives Christian counselling-care its unique dynamic, we must now face the fact that it may quickly become apparent that Martha's relationship with Christ is itself strained or distorted, and we may need to work on that obstacle also as a vital part of 'how' Martha will move towards more abundant living. My instinct is that to describe three types of spiritual obstruction may best make my point.

A. *The obstacle of low spiritual expectation*
I have already had cause in this book to warn of the dangers of unrealistically high expectations (see chapter 2) but now it is time to draw attention to the opposite difficulty: as Martha comes to counselling, she may bring with her an expectation of God which is paralysingly *low*. Martha may well have a very low view of her own worth: low expectations of God go with low self-esteem. Furthermore, the current breakthrough of the Spirit into the churches highlights what a low expectation of God His people have generally had: we Christians have been for much too long now in Acts 12.5–16 mode where the believers were praying for Peter's release from prison but clearly did not expect it to happen (note verse 5 and then verses 14 and 15)! In that particular instance, the Lord freed Peter as much *despite* his comrades' prayer as because of it, but we should not take that to mean that we can therefore presume upon the graciousness of God if what we are offering Him is really unbelief. It is clearly essential that the counsellor and Martha, together with any other Christian involved, agree together to look to the Lord for the power to heal wounds, light the way, motivate healthy change, show Martha new truth and enable her to live by it; it may be that some work will need to be done with Martha to help her to that place spiritually.

B. *The obstacle of self-preoccupation*
To begin with, most counselees are hurting or troubled so that it is natural that they are turned in anxiously upon themselves and their own difficulties. At the outset, therefore, Martha will be thoroughly self-preoccupied. I have a concern

which occasionally crosses the line over into anxiety that an over-emphasis upon or an exalting of counselling itself *induces* or *re-inforces* self-preoccupation: yes, there is a proper self-*concern*, but self-*centredness* is the very antithesis of the gospel which Jesus Christ lived, died and rose again to establish. It does seem to me that self-centredness may very well be the inevitable outcome of secular counselling which has no God and must therefore depend upon and appeal to self-help, self-reliance and self-interest, even if sometimes allied to what one might call a high humanism. (For a valuable and intense critique of the 'self-ism' of secular psychology, read Paul Vitz's book, *Psychology as Religion: the Cult of Self Worship*, Lion, 1977). Much of this 'self-ism' permeates the everyday advice which members of our society offer to one another along the lines of 'you look after yourself', 'you stand up for your rights', and so on, a self-orientation all the more aggravated by the trail-blazers in our society (politicians, advertisers, television 'stars') now often brazenly hailing self-interest as the highway to the good life. All in all, then, it is hardly surprising that, as she presents herself to you, Martha is very self-occupied. You will need to show her that *the* High Way to the Good Life is *Christ*-centredness:

> 'If anyone would come after me, he must deny himself and take up his cross and follow me. For whoever wants to save his life will lose it, but whoever loses his life for me will find it' (Matthew 16.24–25).

Martha will find herself only as she becomes Christ-occupied. As her counsellor representing Christ to her, you and I need to take full responsibility for ensuring that the counselling transaction depends upon and points to our Lord, and we should be looking out for prayer-landmarks, assignments and symbolic actions which magnify Him.

C. *The obstacle of apparently spiritual wishful thinking*
What I have in mind by this heading is that very difficult situation where Martha so very badly wants a particular thing to happen and where it can be argued that God wants that thing to happen too, and therefore she says that it is absolutely bound to happen and soon, whereas the reality is

that, given the prevailing circumstances, the *likelihood* of that thing happening is remote. My wife is an upper school teacher: the capacity of parents tenaciously to hold academic pretensions for their offspring which have no foundation in the reality of classwork, homework and school examinations never ceases to amaze her! There are many Christian equivalents. Here is a Christian man who desperately seeks employment with a caring or Christian agency, and not for economic or career prospects either: actually, there are psychological reasons related to his own needs as to why he so desperately wants that kind of work, and actually he is quite unsuited for it, but all of that is hidden behind a fierce insistence that God wants him to have such a ministry and has told him so, an insistence which defies his fellow-Christians to say otherwise. Here is a Christian woman who so desperately wants her husband to become a Christian that she avows and declares God has the matter in hand: she *knows*, God has told her – only it doesn't happen, and nobody else is surprised that it does not happen: it is not that the arm of the Lord is too short to save but rather that the husband is not one whit interested; the wife has turned an albeit natural and proper desire of her heart into an improper declaration of what God *must* do, and her own being will be stressed by that. I have three adult sons: they are fine young men, healthy, able, great friends together, with excellent work prospects, and all else that matches the modern materialistic yardstick. However, neither Stephen nor David nor Andrew is a Christian. It would be foolish to pretend that that is not a disappointment to me: it is the heaviest I bear. What bothers me, though, is the easy and absolute conviction with which this and then that Christian has declared to me that God has the matter already in hand: 'God says you will have good news *soon*' was the gist of one 'word' delivered to me – only it was delivered years ago. I *hope* that my beloved sons will commit themselves to Christ, I *pray* that they will, I would *love* it to happen for their own sakes (yes, and for mine) but I do not fiercely expect or demand it, because God does not make people Christians until those people turn themselves in the direction of Christ, and there is no indication that my sons have any current intention of doing any such thing. It would be a crippling thing for me to live in eager expectation of their imminent conversion by turning wishful thinking into divine promise. If Martha comes to you for counselling with any such fierce precondition laid at God's door as to what He must do, you will have gently to show her that she has, as it were, tied God's hands behind His back, and that she needs to untie Him so that He may freely minister His grace to her in His way and in His time.

Group work

One further practical possibility to advance the 'how' of counselling is to consider meeting Martha's needs through her incorporation into a group composed of people with similar needs. For example, in our church fellowships there may very well be some whose main difficulties with living are associated with their being single: it is by no means always easy or comfortable to be single in our society, whether 'single' means unmarried, separated, divorced or bereaved, and there may be those who frankly do not want to be single either and who find continuing singleness hard to bear. Two of our fellowship's counsellors, one of whom is herself single by bereavement, pioneered a context in which 'singles' could come together and share their experiencing of singleness. Our counsellors' perception is that the group sessions enabled quite a lot of stress to be unloaded and shared to a degree which might not otherwise have occurred. Furthermore, quite a number of our singles in the 25–40 age-range have developed a pattern of Sunday evening informal open-house meetings, plus a range of week night social activities which are thoroughly therapeutic and enjoyable. This is a further example (see chapter 8 for other examples) of how the Christian community is uniquely placed to take caring initiatives, in this case to *include in* some of those who may feel lonely or marginalized but whom Jesus Christ is always seeking to draw to Himself and into the family fellowship of those who belong to Him and therefore to one another.

The question of when and where

Clearly 'when' has to do with at least two diaries: from the counsellor's point of view, a session is best arranged in a not too busy day, with a little space before and after the time agreed. Counselling is not only important work, it is *hard* work: a little time for preparation beforehand, and afterwards for reflection, for making notes in your own utterly confidential file and for relaxation, is an ideal to aim at. I have already argued for the value of clear arrangements and understandings from the start, but a major time-issue which calls for comment is that of bringing a particular counselling session to a close. Christian carers particularly may find it hard to draw to a close when it is clear that there is much unfinished business so that the temptation is to go for a mammoth session rather than several shorter ones. Actually, overly prolonged counselling sessions can take a serious toll of both counsellor and counselee alike, causing a state of exhaustion which does not advance the counselling cause and may detract from it. Counsellors who cannot end a session more or less when agreed may be revealing more about their own anxiety to help than really helping the counselee. It is helpful to remind Martha of the agreed boundary for each session at the beginning of it and to adhere to that. It is also helpful, and can be very productive, to indicate to Martha when there are about ten minutes of a session remaining: it is often near the end of sessions that counselees reveal important material; what the counsellor should then do is to sum up and intimate that the material just revealed provides a real starting-point for next time – which will be next week, on such and such a day, from 3–4.30pm, at the same location. If possible, in an ongoing counselling situation, sessions should be weekly and the next session should always be firmly established before the conclusion of the present one, so as to give stability and commitment to the counselling relationships.

'Where' should counselling sessions take place? A prime requirement is that the room should be reasonably soundproof and private: there should be no distracting offstage noises coming through the walls and the room should be so positioned that you can converse without feeling that somebody outside may be able to hear what is being said; the only telephone ever to be allowed in a counselling room is an unplugged one and every precaution should be taken to ensure that you will not be disturbed – when in doubt, put a notice on the door. The room itself should be non-threatening: it is not helpful to the counselling process if the counsellor sits in an executive chair behind an imposing desk and under one of those posters depicting, say, a large bull-elephant and bearing some such legend as 'you want to argue?' The room should be comfortable and the placing of chairs neutral, that is to say, there is no ascendancy to be gained by sitting in any particular chair. Chairs should neither be directly facing each other nor so acutely angled that you get a crick in your neck by having to turn your head so far to see the other person: I discover that I naturally place chairs about one and a half metres apart and at an angle of 120 degrees. The counsellor's clothing should be neither too severely formal nor over-casual. It may seem to some that this paragraph is finicky: however, our care in such matters may send a positive signal to Martha and is, in any case, an expression of our genuine concern for her and her wellbeing.

The question of until

How long should a counselling relationship last? It is impossible to answer that question in terms of *time*: it can be answered only in relation to the *goals* of the counselling enterprise. In the fourth paragraph of this chapter, I summarized what we would hope and expect to see happening. A counselling relationship should therefore continue until either there is impasse or breakthrough in relation to the counselling's goals.

Until impasse
All counsellors will encounter situations in which the counselling process is stagnating; there is no perceptible progress towards the goals, and what is required is termination and/ or referral. Termination in such circumstances is always likely to be difficult, especially for Christian counsellors in whom a whole phalanx of negative thoughts and emotions may be aroused. Is not termination another word for rejection? and referral, for abdication? Are not they the very opposites of the Spirit of Jesus Christ? Beneath such questions, guilt and anxiety may flourish. It is fundamental that we counsellors acknowledge and come to terms with counselling failures and, indeed, with our own failings and limitations as counsellors. Only then will we be able to fulfil one of the essential counselling requirements which is *to let go* of our clients when there

is no more worthwhile journeying to be done with them, and to let go of them *for their own sakes*. Jesus let the so-called rich young ruler go. He let go of many disciples and gave even the Twelve opportunity to leave Him (John 6.66–67). More pertinently perhaps, He went away from them when the time had come, His motivation being clear:

'It is for your good that I am going away' (John 16.7).

Whether we reach impasse or breakthrough, we must be able to let people go, remove ourselves, leave people as free agents, free, hopefully, to love and serve the Lord, rejoicing in the power of His Holy Spirit.

There are a number of factors which may contribute to a state of impasse being reached between Martha and me the counsellor: it may be the limitations of my knowledge and experience; Martha may have a personality disorder which it is beyond my present capacity to understand or penetrate; she may be an expert at psychological manipulation beyond my powers of discerning or coping; her whole personality make-up and mine may prove to be so far short of being compatible that we are simply not going to reach the deep places together. For whatever reasons, the counselling relationship is going nowhere and I know it. Stubbornly to continue in such circumstances could prove injurious to both of us. It is time to face with Martha the reality of the impasse and to call a halt. Hopefully, I would have secured her agreement at the start that we would continue for only as long as she and I could maintain that it was fruitful to do so, and I now refer back to that understanding with a view to enabling Martha to accept that the present counselling arrangement has run its course. I shall also seek to underline the gains that have been made. Nevertheless, the termination may be painful: your 'Martha' may well have come to depend upon you and her relationship with you, and, unwilling to lose you, she may 'find' some fresh problems or secrets to lay before you, working upon your guilt-feelings by appealing to you not to abandon her. We Christians, I fear, can be a soft touch and are not always good at sticking to our guns in a context of caring. It is in fact for Martha's own good that we summon up the resolution to bring the counselling relationship to an end even if she attempts to cajole or intimidate us not to do so or even if she melodramatically storms out of the room. It is actually possible that what termination arouses may give her a way ahead and so itself be beneficial but even if the opposite appears to be the case, we must let her go and withdraw ourself when there is nowhere else for us to travel together.

The commonest form of termination is referral – that is to say, to refer Martha to another counsellor whom you have good reason to believe may be able to help her as you yourself no longer can, someone more experienced, more expert, more au fait with her kind of difficulty or personality than you are. In referring, you may have to deal not only with charges of rejection from Martha but with allegations that you yourself lay at your own door to the effect that you are ridding yourself of a 'problem-person'. What we need to develop is a view of referral which is *positive*, which sees referral not as rejection but as *recommendation* in Martha's best interests, so that it becomes not so much indicative of our own inadequacy as of our genuine pastoral insight and care. Martha needs assistance which you cannot now give her but which A. N. Other can. She may need her doctor to prescribe medication and refer her on to specialist help or she may need a specialist Christian counsellor whom you will find through the Christian grapevine. Further food for thought in respect of referral can be garnered from reference counselling books such as Howard Clinebell's *Basic Types of Pastoral Care and Counselling* (see his Chapter 12) and Eugene Kennedy's *On Becoming a Counsellor* (see his chapter 16).

Until breakthrough

It may seem natural to assume that, compared with the problems of termination where there is impasse, termination following substantial progress will be straightforward – but by no means all counselees see it in quite that way! Who *wants* to end an active relationship which is both supportive and fruitful? Or who *wants* to lose a new found 'parent' who cares about you and whom you can trust? As an additional complication, you the counsellor may be tempted on behalf of your own needs to continue a relationship in which you are highly valued. However, if you have Martha's wellbeing to the fore, you are praying and working towards that time when she can take responsibility for her own reactions, attitude, decisions and behaviour without needing to look to you, without blame-shifting or crumpling. Whilst being unable to go all the way with Jay Adams' commitment to confrontation (even a cursory glance at the Concordance shows that the gentler *parakaleo* is far more extensively used in the New Testament than the hardline *noutheteo*), I do nonetheless warmly applaud his vigorous reinstatement of the Biblical truth that human beings are to take responsibility for their own sins and for their own reactions even to events or circumstances which are none of their own making. The fact that jokes about people's irregular behaviour being due to their having been dropped on their heads as babies are now universal only serves to point up how pervasive the *explaining* away of personal responsibility and accountability has become. People do not *have* to blame their parents or curse God; they do not *have* to capitulate to rage, frustration, depression and the like, or be eaten up by bitterness, jealousy, misery and the like; they do not *have* to behave as they do. It is an integral part of the counsellor's responsibility to bring Martha through to that recognition – which *includes* her not *having* to be dependent upon her counsellor.

A crucial insight in respect of termination is that the counsellor should actively prepare the way for it to happen. Once counselling goals are being achieved, the counsellor's strategy of care should gradually change: there should be more emphasis upon those ways in which Martha now copes more effectively and upon past difficulties which she has now surmounted, attitudes and behaviour problems which she has changed, and new insights for living which she has gained. There are reputable counsellors who advocate the writing down of such evidences of significant advance for Martha to keep and refer to for her future encouragement. In this way, it should be possible for a good and fruitful counselling relationship to end by mutual consent, Martha being heartened that you, her counsellor, now trust her to deal effectively and Christianly for herself with the vicissitudes of life.

Termination need not, and preferably should not be, absolute. It is right and good that Martha knows that you are available should future emergencies arise. More than that, our context is that of the Christian church: here again, the local fellowship is uniquely placed to provide the ongoing aftercare which Martha needs. In Christ and in the fellowship of His people she still relates with you, not now as counselee to counsellor but as a fellow member of the Body of Christ, which makes you both co-workers with Christ: to move from the one relating to the other will take some time, effort and prayer, but it is a rich asset. Furthermore, all the goodness of worship with self-offering, preaching, teaching and prophecy, and of close relating and prayer-ministry in the house-group, are rich resources available to her, as is that of her now helping others herself as she draws upon the new insight and testimony counselling has given her. Through the instrumentation of a counsellor-servant of His, and because of the power of His grace through His Son and by His Spirit, the Lord will delight with us to see a Martha who walks through her days a little taller, a little more assuredly, a little more gladly, eyes fixed upon Jesus, a little more in the manner of one who now knows herself to be a beloved and growing daughter of God.

Recommended Reading

Rather than give the sort of bibliography that overwhelms, I have selected just ten books which are germane to the material I have presented; they are by no means all out of the same theological stable, but I believe that most will stand the test of time.

1 Ordering Your Private World: Gordon MacDonald: Highland Books: 1985
Concentrates upon the cultivation of our own inner being by way of our discipline and God's grace; our spiritual integrity is essential to the counselling enterprise.

2 Healing: Francis MacNutt: Ave Maria Press: 1974
Now established as a classic in its field; gives a balanced overview of the nature and the healing of physical, emotional and spiritual sickness.

3 Jesus and the Spirit: James Dunn: S.C.M.: 1975
A magisterial piece of New Testament scholarship which focuses upon the person and the ministry of the Holy Spirit in Jesus and in the New Testament church; requires real application to work through it; fairly liberal; gives a substantial biblical/theological foundation to the whole renewal experience.

Now seven books more specifically geared to the counselling-care task: these increase in the degree of depth into which they go i.e. 4 is easy, 10 is not!

4 Why Am I Afraid to Tell You Who I am? John Powell: Fontana/Collins: 1975
A popularizing description of the roles we act, the masks we wear, the games we play rather than revealing who we really are; a good stimulus for us to get into contact with who we really are ourselves. . . .

5 A Friend in Need: Selwyn Hughes: Kingsway: 1981
A popular manual on caring at the encouragement and exhortation levels – which all Christians can participate in; helpfully takes some of the mystique out of 'counselling.'

6 Who Cares? Evelyn Peterson: Paternoster: 1980
Very good handbook of Christian counselling – by a registered psychotherapist who is also a committed Christian. 'Points for discussion' follow each chapter – good starters for a trainee counsellors' group.

7 Christian Counselling: Gary Collins: Word Publishing: British edition 1985

OR

On Becoming a Counsellor: Eugene Kennedy: Gill and Macmillan: 1977
Very good and comprehensive reference books for non-professional Christian counsellors: Collins covers more life problems and assembles biblical resources; Kennedy includes more on the counsellor himself/herself and on the actual counselling transaction. Both highly recommended.

8 Competent to Counsel: Jay Adams: Baker: 1970

and

9 Basic Types of Pastoral Care and Counselling: Howard Clinebell: S.C.M.: (revised and enlarged) 1984
Deliberate choice of two 'classics' representing very different schools of thought, often in conflict. Adams insistent upon a strictly Biblical basis for all aspects of counselling; advocates confrontational style, strong on right thoughts and behaviour. Clinebell insistent upon inte-

grating secular psychotherapy with Christian counselling practice; advocates a wide range of styles and therapies.

10 Roots and Shoots: Roger Hurding: Hodder and Stoughton: 1986

An invaluable 'map' which traces the development of secular psychologies with their many branch-roads, and then charts the differing ways in which Christian counsellors come to terms with the secular data; includes balanced evaluation of the convictions and styles of Adams and Clinebell (see above!) and many others; indispensable.

P.S. If you find that you are in imminent danger of taking yourself too seriously, then read what, on occasions, I find to be the most therapeutic tome of all! Being. . . .

11 The Sacred Diary of Adrian Plass: Adrian Plass: Marshall Pickering: 1987